GREEN FIRE

GREEN
FIRE

FRANCIS MALLMANN

with Peter Kaminsky and Donna Gelb

Principal photography by William Hereford

ARTISAN

NEW YORK

As a child I learned the language
* of the clouds*
Of the wind, the forest, the trees,
* the lakes.*
The glaciers on the Andes.
Without my knowing it,
This landscape stole inside of me
Never leaving

One day I remembered it all
and, kneeling on the ground,
I picked up these memories
They were my tools
Forged in the still-glowing embers
* of my childhood's hearth*
Together we found my way to
* cook*
Fire, always fire.

Francis Mallmann
La Isla, Patagonia

CONTENTS

INTRODUCTION:
BACK TO THE GARDEN

When I was sixteen, I lived alone in a small house that I rented in Bariloche, the mountain town where I grew up. I chose a special corner behind the cabin for a garden. I readied the ground and put up a low fence to protect my crops from greedy rabbits. I installed a powerful light so that when I rose at five in the morning, I could tend the garden before heading out to my day job at a rental car agency. As gardens go, mine was quite simple: just carrots, parsley, and a few other herbs, but I protected them as if they were a treasure.

Now, nearly fifty years later, and with a lifetime behind the stove, I recall that teenage boy and what I was searching for in my garden: I wanted to understand how things are born and grow, age, and die. Although I didn't truly comprehend it in my youth, that vegetable garden was the beginning of a lifelong quest to unravel the mysteries of life.

For those of you who know my cooking, it may come as a surprise that after so many years of unconditional love for meat that I now ask you to come along with me, back to the garden, and to cook through a book where vegetarian and vegan recipes are the stars. Does this mean that I have given up on charred rib eyes, creamy sweetbreads, and long-roasted lambs on the cross? It does not. But as with many of you, a growing awareness of our era's perils to Nature herself has caused me to consider my cuisine in a new light.

To be sure, as a son of Patagonia, an immense land of panthers and condors, of gauchos tending vast herds of cattle and of indigenous people who hunted llama-like guanacos and choikes (our native ostriches), I don't think I will ever be a full-on vegetarian. Still, if we are to survive on our small blue planet, we have to find a way to a new language of cooking, one that doesn't require us to destroy the rain forest to grow feed for cattle or to imprison animals on factory farms that condemn them to short and brutal lives. Nothing could be more estranged from the environment where these creatures have evolved to thrive and, in so doing, sustain us. I am saddened when I see this, and it has deepened my appreciation for the code of many of my friends who follow a diet of fruits and vegetables, grains and nuts. Although you may find it hard to believe, my favorite meal—judging by how often I eat it—just might be a plate of basmati rice and a red cabbage salad (page 130).

Of course, like any chef, I have always served vegetables, but it's also fair to say they have frequently been more of a sideshow than a main attraction. In this book, they play the leading role in an ongoing journey of rediscovery. My goal is to create meals for vegetarians and vegans that are as sumptuous and satisfying as a succulent T-bone steak or a plump brook trout plucked from a mountain stream. I am as entranced by the crackling crust of a thick slice of potato in clarified butter done on the plancha; the ineffable creaminess of an eggplant roasted in the embers of a campfire; the sprightly sweetness of an overripe tomato, ever so slowly confited in olive oil. The transformations wrought by flames, coals, and smoke on fruits and vegetables are nothing short of alchemy.

In this book, as it has always been for me, my recipes are born in dreams, following no logic other than desire. And just as in dreams, my memories of meals, of family and friends, of mentors, and of lovers take center stage for a moment, and if I am truly listening, they guide me and take shape in the encounter of fire, iron, and food. As time passes, each new arrival in my family of recipes gives birth to a houseful of children and grandchildren . . . and so on. The possibilities border on the infinite. These dreams have blazed a path for me, the path of *green fire*.

This return to the garden is not so much a change of direction for me as it is a profound deepening of a lifelong affection for fire. I hope you draw inspiration from these recipes, but don't, by any means, shy away from taking them down your own path. Use them as a beacon, not a commandment. I have always believed that in order to be a true cook you must surely master technique but, at the same time, stay attuned to your own unique spirit of rebelliousness and irreverence. If you pay attention, this spirit is a fire that burns within all of us.

THE FACES OF FIRE

Things taste better when cooked out-of-doors. "Why?" you ask. I believe that the pleasure of cooking and eating is much more than a matter of ingredients meeting taste buds. In the outdoors, so many other elements come into play: the wind, the scent of pine trees and grass and flowers, the sunset painting the hills. In the presence of fire, these things make us feel more alive and in the moment.

How can one fully describe the primeval attraction of staring at dancing flames? Equally seductive, the aromas of cooking borne aloft by woodsmoke; it is bred within us. It quickens the pulse and soothes the spirit. Even if you don't find yourself in a remote valley in the Andes but in your own backyard, or at a street festival in the city, the union of food and fire somehow summons up all of these feelings in the way that a song evokes the memories of an embrace though years may have passed.

There are many fine chefs who can make gorgeous, complicated recipes, usually with the assistance of a brigade of helpers ready to follow the chef's every command. But even more elegant and pure, to my way of thinking, is the lone cook who can do a simple thing to perfection. Cooking with fire is a loving tutor if you give yourself over to it.

In Patagonia, we usually build a fire on the ground under a grate or plancha (griddle), then rake the coals to pile them up for more heat or to spread them out for less. Often, we will have a campfire on the side to replenish our coals for long-cooked recipes. For safety, I like to surround this fire with a ring of stones. This age-old method is exceedingly low-tech, but once you learn to listen to the language of fire you will find that you can adjust the heat of wood fire almost as effectively as turning a knob on your home oven. If you want more heat, then add more coals. For less heat, let the coals burn down or rake some aside. True, you can't set a wood fire to be exactly 325°F (170°C)—but honestly, the ingredients won't know the difference if the heat of your fire is a few degrees above or below. Cooking is not all that scientifically precise. Rather than adjusting heat by the marks on a dial, in fire cookery I think in terms of a sliding scale from high all the way down to very low. Thankfully, we are born with a built-in temperature gauge: our hands. If you hold your palm at a safe distance from the fire or cooking surface, you can feel the difference between intense, moderate, and gentle heat. No dials, gauges, or thermometers required. No special equipment needed. In short, less is more.

You will quickly get a sense of how hot a fire is. Start by holding your hand about 4 inches (10 cm) above the cooking surface and counting. When it is too hot after two full seconds, that is high heat. Using the same "now it feels too hot" method, the chart below is a good guideline for gauging heat from a fire. Bear in mind that all of us have different sensitivity to heat.

2 seconds: high heat
3 to 4 seconds: medium-high heat
5 to 6 seconds: medium heat
7 to 8 seconds: medium-low heat
8 to 12 seconds: very low heat

Don't rush your count. You want full seconds. We Argentines count "un matador, dos matador," etc. In English, go with "one Mississippi, two Mississippi."

MY GREEN FIRE

I suppose that the first grillers at the dawn of time cooked their food by impaling it on a stick and holding it over a flame. Although this is a fine method for roasting marshmallows or a hot dog, humanity has perfected better ways to get the most satisfaction from the encounter of food and fire. From direct radiant heat over coals to warmth diffused through iron, to heat trapped within the walls of an oven or transferred to a cauldron.

When cooking with wood, be sure to use hardwoods such as oak, maple, cherry, apple, or hickory. They don't burn down to ashes as quickly as softer woods. Pine, fir, and eucalyptus all impart unpleasant flavors. You can also use charcoal, but, whenever possible, I like the experience of lighting a fire, staring into the flames, losing myself in daydreams and anticipation. Then, when the coals are ready, so am I.

If it's not practical to cook over a wood fire, I prefer lump charcoal. Part of the romance of cooking with fire is the jumbled-up appearance of the embers and coals. But if charcoal briquets are all that you can find, they will work, too.

For safety, always have a bucket of water, a shovel, some dirt or sand, and a fire extinguisher handy, just in case.

PLANCHA

My plancha looks like a cast-iron coffee table. I cook on it more frequently than I cook by any other method. (For many of these recipes, a griddle or skillet placed on top of a grill grate will work well.) The advantage of a large cooking area means you can heat different parts of it to different temperatures—in a way, if you manage your fire well, a plancha can serve the same purpose as multiple burners on a stove. You can sear things over high heat such as Charred Tomatoes with Garlic and Thyme (page 70), or slowly cook a thick slice of breaded eggplant until you create a crackling crust and a creamy inside (Eggplant Milanesa, page 83). You can adjust the heat by adding more wood and coals under one part of the plancha while letting coals burn down to glowing embers or ashes under another part. Once you have your fire going and the plancha warmed, you can quickly increase the temperature by throwing some kindling on the coals and allowing the flames to lick the bottom of the plancha.

One of the virtues of cast iron is that it heats evenly and retains the heat. This is because of its thickness as well as the nature of iron. Whether you cook indoors or out, give your cast iron up to ten minutes to preheat.

Although a cast-iron griddle or large skillet (such as those made by Lodge and Weber) will serve in place of a plancha over the grate of a Weber kettle, I prefer the plancha's larger surface so that I can have access to a range of cooking

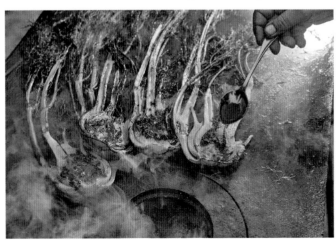

temperatures. I even like an area with no heat under it where I can move things if I want to slow down or stop the cooking.

If there is someone in your area who makes wrought-iron doors, gates, or fences, you could have them make you a plancha about 30 by 30 inches (76 cm) on four legs, 12 to 15 inches (30 to 38 cm) tall.

CALDERO

The literal translation of the Spanish *caldero* is "cauldron"—a fine word, but for most English speakers, this conjures up images of witches stirring a bubbling pot of toadstools, frogs, and snakes. A more familiar term might be "Dutch oven": a high-sided unenameled cast-iron pot (with a lid) that I use for boiling, deep-frying, braising, and baking. You can set it on a grate over coals that range from high heat to gentle warming. To prevent the hot oil from igniting, the bed of coals under the caldero should be slightly smaller in area than the caldero itself. You can also put the caldero off to one side of your fire to keep things warm. For soups and beans, a caldero is a must.

Always use extreme caution when deep-frying—this is just as critical when frying outdoors

in a caldero. Flying sparks or embers can ignite the oil, resulting in a dangerous fire.

Keep in mind that any recipe that calls for a caldero can be cooked indoors in a Dutch oven.

PARRILLA

A parrilla is the most common fire-cooking grill in Argentina. At its simplest, it's a grill grate placed over coals. You can cook directly on the parrilla or set a skillet or Dutch oven on top of the grate.

You can easily construct an Argentine-style parrilla with a few cinder blocks and a grate. Or you can have one like mine made, 36 by 30 inches (91 by 76 cm) and about 9 inches (23 cm) high. I like the generosity of space of this size parrilla. It allows a good amount of room for whatever you are cooking. If you crowd vegetables, they will steam and soften rather than crisp and char. Whether you use wood or charcoal, I find that the optimum time to grill on the parrilla is when the hot coals are covered over with white ash.

HORNO

Cooking in an horno adds a distinct but never overpowering touch of smokiness to any ingredient. These wood-fired ovens have become more popular and more affordable in the years since I wrote *Seven Fires*. They are versatile. By adding more wood, you can crank them up to superhot temperatures for quick, intense roasting. Or you can let the fire burn down to coals for slower roasting in gentle overall heat. Move the food closer to the fire in the back of the stove for greater radiant heat, or place the food right at the entrance for the same radiant heat without blast-furnace temperatures. In time you will learn to gauge temperature by looking at your fire. As a rough guide, an inexpensive infrared

oven thermometer will get you in the zone. You will need a peel, like they use in pizzerias or bread bakeries, to place food in the oven and to move it around to the right cooking spots. For those of you without your own wood-burning oven, each recipe offers temperatures and timings for a conventional oven.

RESCOLDO

I learned this method from Patagonia's cowboys—gauchos—who would often bury a few potatoes in the warm embers and ashes of their breakfast fire and leave them to cook while they were off with their horses. All it requires are the remains of a fire and whatever ingredient you are cooking—pumpkin, squash, beets, potatoes. With all rescoldo cooking, you want a mix of warm ashes and some glowing embers—even a few coals—covering your ingredients so they char slowly on the outside as the insides cook through. You may need to add some embers and coals from time to time to manage the subtle warmth of this method.

"But won't your food taste of ashes?" people often ask. If you dust off the ingredients well and peel the skins, there are no ashes to speak of. There is an old Irish folk saying: "You have to eat a peck of dirt before you die." I feel the same about ashes.

Your Weber Kettle
Is an All-Purpose Grill

In my travels in the United States, the type of fire cookery I have seen most often is on the familiar Weber kettle grill. You light the fire and wait for the coals to die down, then you have about twenty minutes to do your cooking before the temperature is no longer in the sweet spot. Practically speaking, this commonly used method makes it difficult to adjust the heat or easily add coals. However, with a few accessories available from Weber (see Resources, page 303), you can utilize their kettle quite well for the recipes in this book. Any cast-iron skillet or griddle on top of Weber's grill grate will serve you well for many of the recipes; a hinged grate with a removable center piece will allow you to add coals directly under a plancha to raise the heat. A pair of char baskets placed inside the perimeter of the grill will let you add coals to either side of the kettle so that it can work as an horno (oven). You can use an old-fashioned (not digital) meat thermometer stuck in the holes on top of the Weber to monitor temperature. Or, if you are addicted to tech, there are digital probes that can interface with your phone (see Resources, page 303). Long-handled tongs and grilling gloves or oven mitts are the best way to avoid burns when handling food on the grill, moving pots and pans, or lifting the removable center piece or hinged grate.

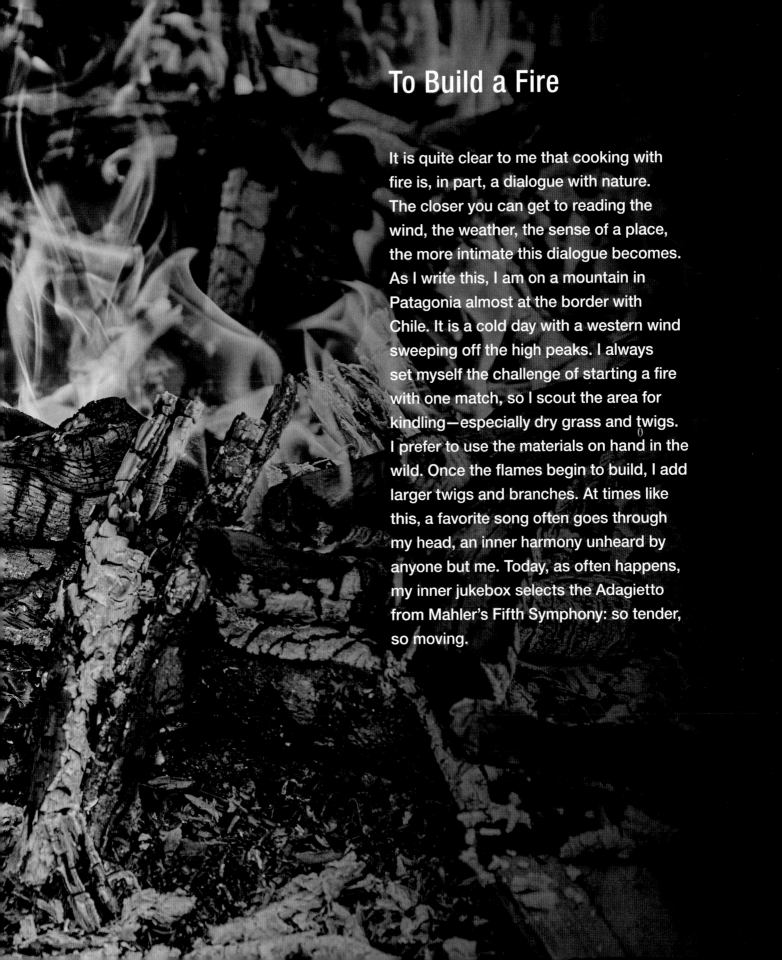

To Build a Fire

It is quite clear to me that cooking with
fire is, in part, a dialogue with nature.
The closer you can get to reading the
wind, the weather, the sense of a place,
the more intimate this dialogue becomes.
As I write this, I am on a mountain in
Patagonia almost at the border with
Chile. It is a cold day with a western wind
sweeping off the high peaks. I always
set myself the challenge of starting a fire
with one match, so I scout the area for
kindling—especially dry grass and twigs.
I prefer to use the materials on hand in the
wild. Once the flames begin to build, I add
larger twigs and branches. At times like
this, a favorite song often goes through
my head, an inner harmony unheard by
anyone but me. Today, as often happens,
my inner jukebox selects the Adagietto
from Mahler's Fifth Symphony: so tender,
so moving.

POTATOES

A DEBT OF GRATITUDE

In a way, I could say that potatoes—the great gift of the Andes—marked the turning point in my career. I realized this in 1995. My career was moving along nicely. I had already run a successful cooking school and enjoyed a devoted following on television. Along the way, I'd started a few restaurants that did quite well, although like everyone in my country, I was buffeted by the economic and political winds that came and went. Back home in Patagonia, I cooked simply and with fire, but in sophisticated Buenos Aires, my restaurant food was more an Argentine version of fancy European cuisine.

I was a bit bored.

And then the hand of Providence (and potatoes) entered when I was informed that I had received the Grand Prize of the prestigious International Academy of Gastronomy—the first South American to be recognized by a group that has bestowed this honor on such cooking legends as Alain Ducasse and Ferran Adrià.

What shall I make for this assembly of dining demigods? I wondered. Surely they hadn't turned to me to see what I could do with lobster Thermidor or foie gras. There was nothing particularly South American about that kind of food, and I had been invited, I believed, because I was particularly South American. Then, in a moment of reflection, a thought stirred in my soul: one word . . . *potatoes.*

To any son or daughter of Patagonia, this humble tuber, dug out of the dirt, is the food that has united the cuisines of the peoples who live in the shadow of the Andes: from the shores of Tierra del Fuego to the highlands of Peru. To this day, the Incas leave potatoes out to freeze in the frigid mountain air, then thaw them in the blazing sun (a very low-tech way of freeze-drying). Closer to my childhood home in Bariloche, the ancient Mapuche people would cook them curanto-style: buried in rock-and-earth-filled firepits along with leg of llama and ears of corn in their husks. After their morning meal on the pampas, gauchos would toss a few potatoes into the ashes of their campfire to cook slowly (in the style we call rescoldo) until they reached smoky creaminess, perhaps to serve at lunch with a lashing of chimichurri. And of course, my mother knew that her crisp and golden french fries could tame the appetites of her rambunctious sons.

For my Grand Prix meal, I resolved to showcase potatoes for the gathered gastronomers in the fairy-tale castle of the Hotel Schloss outside Frankfurt, Germany. To set the plan in motion, I sent my second-in-command Germán Martitegui (who is now a world-renowned chef) to Cuzco, the ancient royal capital of the Incas. His mission: to buy a thousand pounds of Andean potatoes, chosen from the endless varieties in the town market: red, yellow, orange, purple.

The dinner was an enormous success. The president of the academy pronounced it "Food made by the angels!"

That experience had a life-changing effect on me. I resolved at that moment to simplify my food and to embrace the Patagonian heritage of wood-fire cooking. Out went the complicated sauces, the vegetables diced to the girth of a helium atom, the ornate compositions that left you wondering if you were being asked to eat the entrée put before you or have it framed and hung in a museum. I returned to the fiery roots of Andean cooking. And I have devoted myself to them ever since.

To the potato, then, I owe a great debt of thanks.

MENU

Smashed Andean Yellow Potato with Caviar

Causa Limeña with Avocado and Tomato
(composed Peruvian potato salad with chilies, avocado, and tomato)

Salmon Confit in Potato

Mashed Potato with Confits of Lamb, Duck, and Langoustine

Potato and Mascarpone Soufflé with Berries, Mint, and Pepper

Potato Ice cream with Oranges and Plums

SMASHED POTATOES, FOUR WAYS

This is one of my longtime signature dishes. The flattened-out surface area of a smashed potato allows for lots of crunch as it crisps on the plancha. Sometimes I do nothing more than boil the potato, smash it, and crisp it. It's lovely after a final crisping with a paste of herbs and spices (see the variations that follow).

Small-to-medium Idaho potatoes (russets) work best because they are quite starchy and hold their shape when you smash them. You'll notice that I add oil and vinegar to the boiling liquid. I find that the resulting taste and texture are quite exquisite. If your potatoes crumble apart around the edges when you smash them, just squeeze them back together. You can boil and crisp them ahead of time and then re-crisp on the plancha (or in the oven) just before serving.

The toppings on pages 28–29 are ones that I often use, but if you can imagine some other rubs, pastes, or coatings . . . go for it. When using pastes or rubs, crisp the potatoes on both sides as in the main recipe. Spread a spoonful of the paste or rub on top of the potatoes, then flip them back onto the oiled hot plancha for a minute or two, being careful not to burn the spices. Flip them back onto a plate for serving, spiced side up.

Serves 4

4 medium russet potatoes, scrubbed

Coarse salt

2 tablespoons red wine vinegar

6 tablespoons extra-virgin olive oil, plus more for the pan and plancha

1 bay leaf

¼ teaspoon whole black peppercorns

2 tablespoons unsalted butter, or more as needed, cut into pieces (optional)

Fleur de sel

Prepare a fire for medium-high heat and warm the plancha. (Or pull out a large cast-iron griddle if cooking indoors.)

Meanwhile, place the potatoes in a large pot, cover them with plenty of cold water, and salt the water. Add the vinegar, 2 tablespoons of the olive oil, the bay leaf, and the peppercorns. Bring to a boil, then adjust the heat so the potatoes bubble gently for about 15 minutes, or until the potatoes are tender all the way through when pierced with a skewer. Drain in a colander and set aside until cool enough to handle, but don't allow them to thoroughly cool or they will break instead of smash.

Oil a sheet pan. Place a warm potato on a clean dish towel on a flat work surface. Cover with another clean dish towel. With the palm of your hand, slowly and evenly flatten the potato between the towels. Using a wide sharp-edged spatula, transfer the potato to the prepared sheet pan and repeat with the remaining potatoes. Spoon the remaining 4 tablespoons olive oil evenly over the potatoes.

Brush the hot plancha with olive oil (if cooking indoors, heat the griddle over medium-high heat, then brush with oil). When the oil shimmers, carefully flip the potatoes onto the surface, oiled side down, and cook without moving them until the bottom is crisp, about 5 minutes. Transfer back to the oiled sheet pan, and brush the tops with olive oil.

Brush the hot plancha or griddle with more oil. Slide the spatula under a crisped potato and, with one quick move, flip the potato onto the plancha to cook the other side. Repeat with the remaining potatoes, moving them as little as possible as they cook. At this point, you can drizzle more oil or add dots of butter around the potatoes to help the crisping. It should take 5 to 7 minutes to get them nice and crisp. As they are done, flip them back over onto a serving platter, sprinkle with fleur de sel, and serve immediately.

VARIATIONS

GRIDDLED PEPPERS

Blistered peppers from the Spanish town of Padrón have long been popular as a tapa. The fun is guessing which one of the mostly mild peppers will be the occasional spicy one. More recently, blistered shishito peppers, with similar qualities but easier to come by, have appeared on menus everywhere. Here we have a combination of sliced shishitos and sweet mild peppers tossed with lemon zest, giving these potatoes some powerful jabs of flavor and color.

Serves 4

2 ounces small sweet peppers or shishitos

¼ cup (13 g) chopped fresh parsley leaves

1 teaspoon grated lemon zest

While the potatoes are crisping, slice the peppers and brown them on the hot oiled plancha or griddle. Season them with the parsley and lemon zest and spoon them on top of the crisped potatoes.

TURMERIC, CARDAMOM, CORIANDER, AND ALMOND GREMOLATA

Inspired by spice mixes of the Middle East, North Africa, and India, these flavors are strong, bright, and distinct. If you have a lonely spice mix in your cabinet that you don't know what to do with, moisten it with some olive oil and give it a try.

Serves 4

1 teaspoon cardamom seeds (from a heaping tablespoon of whole pods), crushed

1 teaspoon coriander seeds, crushed

1 tablespoon ground turmeric

1 teaspoon chopped garlic

2 tablespoons chopped almonds

3 tablespoons vegetable oil

Coarse salt

Crush the spices and garlic together in a mortar. Stir in the almonds, crushing them a little but not completely, and stir in enough of the vegetable oil to make a paste. Add salt to taste.

While the potatoes are crisping, spread a spoonful of the spice paste on top. Flip them spiced side down and cook just until the spice paste is fragrant and crisped, 1 to 2 minutes, being careful not to burn the spices. Flip them back onto a plate for serving, spiced side up.

FENNEL POLLEN, FENNEL SEED, ROSEMARY, AND GARLIC

One of the true glories of Italian street food is this seasoning mixture rolled up inside roast pork (porchetta), but there's no reason vegetables can't benefit from this powerful combination as well. The fennel pollen makes this recipe. It pulls everything in the paste into a softly aromatic cloak with a beautiful color.

Serves 4

1 tablespoon chopped fresh rosemary leaves

1 tablespoon fennel seeds

2 tablespoons fennel pollen

1 tablespoon chopped garlic

Extra-virgin olive oil

Crush the rosemary, fennel seeds, fennel pollen, and garlic together in a mortar. Stir in enough olive oil to make a thick, spreadable paste.

While the potatoes are crisping, spread a spoonful of the spice paste on top. Flip them spiced side down and cook just until the spices are fragrant and crisped, 1 to 2 minutes, being careful not to burn the spices. Flip them onto a plate for serving, spiced side up.

PLANCHA POTATO ROUNDS

Many people think that cooking with fire requires the raging heat of a blast furnace, when in fact, the steady heat of a low fire can seduce subtle flavor and texture out of just a few ingredients. Boiling a potato, then griddling it as slowly as a rosebud opening in the sunlight—or so it seemed to me when I was a boy—was the secret in my grandma Tata's kitchen. (Her actual name was Mercedes Sanchez Ponce de Leon.) Here I cut a boiled potato into little steaks, and the almost magical union of potato, plancha, and butter creates the most delicious and elegant crust you can imagine.

Serves 4

4 medium russet potatoes, scrubbed

Coarse salt

Extra-virgin olive oil, for the plancha

4 tablespoons unsalted butter, cut into small pieces

Fleur de sel

Prepare a fire for medium-low heat and warm the plancha. (Or pull out one or more large cast-iron griddles or skillets if cooking indoors.)

Put the whole potatoes in a deep saucepan, cover them with plenty of cold water, add salt, and bring to a boil over medium-high heat. Reduce the heat and let the potatoes bubble gently for about 12 minutes, until they are tender when pierced but still quite firm. Drain and slice the potatoes into rounds about ½ inch (1.25 cm) thick.

Brush the hot plancha with oil (if cooking indoors, heat the griddle over medium-low heat, then brush with oil). When the oil shimmers, add

the potatoes in a single uncrowded layer. Take half the butter and dot it in between the potatoes and around the edges so that it melts into the potatoes as they brown. Cook for about 5 minutes. Turn the potatoes over, dot the plancha or griddle with the remaining butter, and brown the other side, another 3 to 5 minutes. Sprinkle with fleur de sel and serve immediately.

BLACKJACK POTATOES

A few years ago, I was filming a show on the Chilean side of the Andes in a remote and windy spot where the only neighbors were the occasional Andean condors—giant birds that threw a shadow like single-engine airplanes as they glided and swooped overhead. My equipment was about as low-tech as you could find: just a plancha with a fire alongside and a tree branch to help me tip the chapa (another word for a plancha) to let the grease run off. We call these Blackjack Potatoes because the way you lay the thin potato slices down on the plancha reminds me of the way card dealers in a casino deal a hand in blackjack. Reducing cream with sautéed onion and sage creates a velvety and savory coating for the potatoes.

Serves 4

About 6 tablespoons extra-virgin olive oil, plus more if needed

1 onion, thinly sliced

1½ pounds (680 g) russet potatoes, scrubbed and thinly sliced on a mandoline

2 garlic cloves, minced

6 large fresh sage leaves, roughly torn

¼ cup (59 ml) heavy cream

Coarse salt and freshly ground black pepper

Prepare a fire for medium-low heat and warm the plancha. If cooking indoors, heat a large cast-iron griddle or skillet over medium-low heat.

Brush the plancha or griddle with the olive oil and add the onion slices, spreading them out on the hot surface. Add another tablespoon or so of olive oil and cook, turning occasionally, until the onion is golden brown, about 5 minutes. Transfer to a plate and set aside.

Meanwhile, oil another area of the plancha (or a separate griddle) and line a sheet pan with paper towels.

One at a time, in batches if necessary, add the potato slices just like a card dealer at a blackjack table, so that every slice is fully in contact with the hot surface. The thin potatoes will quickly become translucent and you'll see the slices bubbling in the center. After 4 to 5 minutes, when they start to brown, turn the slices over and cook for several minutes longer, until the potatoes are golden and cooked through, with large patches of crispy brown. Transfer them to the prepared sheet pan as they are done. Add more olive oil to the plancha as needed.

Return the onion to the plancha or skillet and add the garlic, sage, and cream, scraping the cream into the onion until it thickens slightly. The aroma of garlic and sage will be quite seductive. Add the potatoes and cook for a minute or so, tossing with the onion. Season to taste with salt and pepper. Using two wide spatulas, transfer it all to a platter and serve immediately.

The Personalities of Potatoes

If you look at potatoes with an aesthetic eye, I'd have to say there is not much to draw the contemplation of an art lover. They're lumpy, irregular in shape, and covered with dirt. I suppose when something spends its life underground, there's no need for brilliant colors or a seductive shape. But when you cook a potato, there is plenty of opportunity for artistry. A cooked potato can be crisp, crunchy, and creamy. It can soak up smoke, salt, oil, butter, pepper, garlic, and the essence of herbs and spices. Even more miraculously, a potato can do all of these things at the same time in a single recipe.

It is this multiple personality side of potatoes that has always spurred me to explore new ways to bring out their many qualities when cooking with fire. Bakers often talk about the relationship of crust to crumb. A baguette has a lot of crust compared to how much airy crumb there is inside, and a dinner roll even more so, while a country bread has a softer and more spacious crumb. Likewise, a french-fried potato has a lot of crust, and a potato chip has even more, while my smashed potatoes (see page 27) have creamy insides but enough crust to satisfy the universal human love of crispiness. Over the years, I have found that by experimenting with shape and with the arrangement of potato pieces on a plancha or in an oven or kettle, you can produce endless variations on the arc of crispy to creamy. Go ahead and play with your potatoes.

RÖSTI WITH RACLETTE

If I asked you to name a favorite food from Switzerland, you might say Swiss cheese or hot chocolate, which are, of course, quite wonderful. For me, though, the roughly grated potato pancake known as rösti takes the prize. In my childhood, it was a favorite when the snowdrifts in our mountain town of Bariloche seemed as tall as horses and my brother and I would come in from whatever snowy games we were playing. In my home today, I often serve it alongside a crisp salad of radicchio and endive with a sharp mustardy vinaigrette.

Grate the potatoes just before you put them on the plancha, then serve the hot and crispy rösti topped with melted cheese. Raclette is both the name of this recipe and the type of cheese we'd often have for an après-ski lunch in Bariloche, and I prefer it, but any mildly pungent cheese (Gruyère, Comté) will work.

Note: The trick to getting the rösti potatoes just right is to find that low-heat bliss point where the inside of the pancake cooks and the outside crisps. If the fire is too strong, you'll get a crispy crust and raw insides. Go low!

Makes 1 large rösti (serves 4)

4 medium russet potatoes, peeled

Extra-virgin olive oil

4 tablespoons unsalted butter, cut into pieces, plus more if needed

2 tablespoons sliced scallions

4 medium endives, trimmed

1 head radicchio, trimmed and halved

My Basic Vinaigrette (page 292)

1 large wedge Raclette (at least 12 ounces/350 g)

Prepare a fire for medium-low heat and warm the plancha. If cooking indoors, heat a large cast-iron griddle or skillet over medium-low heat.

Grate the potatoes. Blot them dry.

Generously oil the hot plancha or griddle. Melt 2 tablespoons of the butter on the hot surface and pile the potatoes onto the buttered plancha or griddle. With a wide spatula, gently flatten them down into an even layer about ¾ inch (2 cm) thick. Cook very gently until a deep golden crust forms on the bottom, about 12 minutes, pressing down on the potatoes now and then. Add a few more dots of butter around the edges if it seems like a good idea. Loosen the rösti with the spatula, slide it onto a large flat plate or rimless baking sheet, and melt the remaining 2 tablespoons butter on the hot plancha or griddle. Cover the rösti with another large plate and invert it onto the buttered plancha to cook the other side for 10 to 12 minutes. When it's perfectly crusted on the bottom and cooked through inside, slide it onto a platter and keep it warm. Scatter the scallions over the rösti.

While the rösti is cooking, slice the endives and radicchio into wide ribbons and place in a salad bowl. Just before serving, toss the salad with the vinaigrette.

To serve, gradually melt the cheese in front of the fire, scraping it down onto the potatoes with the spatula. If cooking indoors, cut the cheese into thick slices and use a separate cast-iron skillet or griddle to slowly melt it.

Cut the rösti into wedges at the table and serve the salad alongside.

BROKEN AND DEEP-FRIED POTATOES

A boiled potato is smooth on the palate. A french fry is all about crispiness. This recipe is about both. First, I boil the potatoes, then chip and break them apart, then I fry them. By breaking a potato apart, you get hundreds of little crevices to crisp up. All these mini ridges and valleys in the broken-up potato create a chorus line of crispiness followed by soft creaminess as you bite down: truly the best of both worlds.

Serves 4

4 medium russet potatoes, scrubbed

Coarse salt

About 8 cups (2 L) oil (preferably a combination of olive and vegetable oils), for deep-frying

Fleur de sel

1 bunch chives, minced

Lemon wedges, for serving

Prepare a fire for medium heat and set a grate over it. Pull out a large deep cast-iron pot, such as a caldero or Dutch oven.

Meanwhile, put the potatoes in another pot, cover them with plenty of cold water, and add salt. Line a sheet pan with a clean dish towel. Bring the water to a boil, then boil the potatoes gently over medium heat for about 12 minutes, until they are tender but still firm. Drain and pat them dry, then set them on the prepared sheet pan until they are cool enough to handle. With the point of a small knife, chip and break the potatoes apart into rough-sided but evenly sized chunks—an inch (2.5 cm) or a bit larger. Once chunked, let them dry further for about 15 minutes.

Line a second sheet pan with paper towels and have ready a long-handled spider or skimmer. Line a serving bowl with a napkin.

Pour enough oil into the caldero or deep cast-iron pot to fill it no more than halfway to the top. Heat the oil on the grate (or on the stovetop over medium heat) until a thermometer reads 350°F (180°C), or until the oil hisses and bubbles around a small piece of potato dropped in as a test.

Add the potatoes, a small uncrowded batch at a time, and fry for 1 to 2 minutes, until they are golden brown and very crunchy. Try to keep the oil up to temperature so the potatoes crisp without becoming heavy, but don't let them burn. As the potatoes are done, lift them out with the spider and transfer to the paper towels to thoroughly drain. Once drained, transfer the potatoes to the napkin-lined bowl, season to taste with fleur de sel, and scatter the chives over them. Serve immediately, with lemon wedges alongside for squeezing over the top.

CRISPY POTATO STRIPS AND PARSLEY SALAD WITH GARLIC CREAM

This idea was born one afternoon when I found myself wandering around Greenwich Village in Manhattan—a charming neighborhood of low-rise buildings that, in spite of its becoming a mecca for the fashionable set, retains much of the flavor of the Italian immigrants who settled there more than a century ago. Simple storefront restaurants are still the rule here. One of my favorites is Mary's Fish Camp. I adore their french fries, lightly dressed with vinegar. I had those piquant potatoes in mind when I dreamed up this salad. In contrast to the many versions of potato salad that you can make well in advance, this salad wants to be eaten right away, while the herbs are fresh and the potatoes are crunchy and cradled in garlicky cream.

Serves 4

½ cup (118 ml) heavy cream
1 teaspoon finely minced garlic
2 large russet potatoes, scrubbed
Olive oil, for deep-frying
2 cups (60 g) fresh parsley leaves
Red wine vinegar
Fleur de sel

Prepare a fire for medium heat and set a grate over it. Pull out a large deep cast-iron pot, such as a caldero or Dutch oven.

Combine the cream with the garlic in a very small saucepan and cook over medium heat until reduced by half. Pour the mixture into a bowl and let cool.

Trim the potatoes into bricks (see page 42), cut them crosswise in half, then slice them lengthwise into very thin strips. They should be about ⅛ inch (3 mm) thick, ¾ inch (2 cm) wide, and 2 to 3 inches (5 to 7 cm) long. Reserve them in a bowl of cold water if you are slicing them ahead of time, but drain them and thoroughly blot them dry on a dish towel before they go into the hot oil.

Pour oil into the caldero or deep cast-iron pot to fill it no more than halfway up the sides and attach a frying thermometer to the side. Set the caldero or pot on the grate (or if cooking indoors, set it on the stovetop over medium heat). Line a sheet pan with paper towels and set it nearby to drain the cooked potatoes. When the oil is hot enough to hiss and bubble around a strip of potato (about 350°F/180°C), carefully add a large handful of the potatoes and fry until they are golden brown and crisp, about 2 minutes. Be careful not to let the oil get too hot, or they will burn very quickly. If they clump together, move them apart with a long-handled spider or skimmer. As the potatoes are done, use the spider to transfer them to the paper towels to drain.

Meanwhile, add the parsley to the garlic cream and toss to coat.

When the potatoes are done, sprinkle them with vinegar to taste, then gently layer them on a platter or individual plates with the dressed parsley. Gently toss the layers together with your hands to lightly dress the potatoes without breaking them. Sprinkle with fleur de sel and serve immediately.

LIFE ON THE EDGE:
POTATO BRICKS AND PYRAMIDS

When you dig a potato from the ground, its shape is basically no shape at all—just a lump. But when you trim it in the style of a brick or pyramid (see page 45), you get flat surfaces—facets—and edges. If you cook potatoes very slowly in an oven, the edges crisp up, the flat surfaces turn many shades of gold and brown, and the inside becomes crumbly. The result, in one recipe, is the entire potato spectrum of color and texture. These bricks are an homage to my grandma Tata, although she never bothered to trim potatoes so precisely. I guess the technique is just my naturally rebellious instinct imposing order on the chaos of potato shapes. Lately I have also been trimming the potatoes into a pyramid shape when the spirit moves. I like to

play with shapes, and I always look for a way to introduce a clash of aesthetics, tastes, and textures in the experience of a meal—a little bit of Wagner on top of a Mozart melody, so to speak. No fork is required, by the way; these potatoes are best eaten by hand.

Notes:
- *Peeled potatoes can be held in a bowl of cold water to cover in the fridge for a day or more. You can also cook the potatoes halfway a few hours before serving and finish them just before you're ready to eat.*
- *To make this recipe vegan, coat and baste with olive oil, not butter.*

POTATO BRICKS

Serves 4

4 large russet potatoes, scrubbed

1 cup (237 ml) Clarified Butter (page 298) or extra-virgin olive oil, plus more if needed

1 bunch chives, chopped

Fleur de sel

Heat the horno, or a home oven, to 375°F (190°C).

Set a potato on its side on a flat work surface and slice off the ends. Then slice off the four sides completely flat to form a brick. Pare off any remaining skin. Cut the brick

crosswise in half and slice each half lengthwise into two symmetrical bricks to get four bricks from each potato. Place them in a large bowl of cold water and repeat with the remaining potatoes.

Drain the bricks and pat them thoroughly dry. Dry the bowl, put the butter or oil in it, and add the potato bricks, turning them so they are thoroughly coated on all sides. Line them up on a sheet pan in rows about an inch (2.5 cm) apart and bake for about 40 minutes, until the potato bricks are nicely browned on the edges and tender inside. Halfway through, rotate the pan

and give it a little shake to loosen any potatoes that are sticking, and baste with more butter or oil from the bowl. If cooking indoors, increase the oven temperature toward the end of the cooking time, if necessary, and use convection, to encourage deeper browning,

Transfer the potato bricks to a serving platter and sprinkle them with chives and fleur de sel.

PYRAMIDS

Cutting potatoes into pyramids is more work than cutting them into bricks, but you get a more dramatic presentation. The trimmings can be roasted separately in a pan with olive oil, garlic, and herbs as a treat for the cook.

Serves 4

12 medium russet potatoes

1 cup (237 ml) Clarified Butter (page 298) or extra-virgin olive oil, plus more if needed

2 tablespoons fresh thyme leaves

Fleur de sel

Heat the horno, or a home oven, to 375°F (190°C).

Set a potato on its side on a flat work surface and slice off the ends. Then slice off the four sides completely flat to form a brick. Starting from one narrow end of the brick, make angled lengthwise cuts to form a four-sided pyramid (see the photos on page 43) and place the trimmed pyramid in a large bowl of cold water so it doesn't discolor. If you'll be using the trimmings, keep them in a separate bowl of water. Repeat with the remaining potatoes.

When the oven is hot, drain the potatoes and thoroughly dry them and the emptied bowl. Add the butter or olive oil and thyme to the bowl, and, with your hands, gently toss the potato pyramids in the mixture until they are completely coated.

Stand the potatoes in uncrowded rows on a sheet pan. Baste them generously with the remaining butter or oil from the bowl, and sprinkle with fleur de sel to taste. Bake for about 1 hour, rotating the pan occasionally and adding more butter or oil as needed, until the potatoes are tender inside and the edges are well browned and very crisp. If necessary, you can move the potatoes closer to the fire toward the end of the cooking time for better browning. If cooking indoors, increase the oven temperature toward the end of the cooking time, if necessary, or use convection, to encourage deeper browning.

HUEVOS A LA TRIPA

This is my wood-fire version of a classic French comfort food that my mom used to make in Bariloche. I served it in my first restaurant there when I was nineteen years old. Don't be alarmed by the word *tripa*, which seems like an oxymoron in a vegetarian book. *Tripa* means "tripe" in Spanish, but in this recipe it refers to the soft and sinewy texture of the strips of onion. I highly recommend eating this dish by the woodstove after a few hours of cross-country skiing, accompanied by a glass of white wine. It is a bit of a gamble as to whether the yolks will still be runny when the casserole is cut into. If they are cooked through, it's still delicious. If they are soft, though, it is divine.

Serves 4

4 large russet potatoes, peeled and cut into
6 pieces each

Coarse salt

3 tablespoons unsalted butter

Freshly ground black pepper

Freshly grated nutmeg

1 tablespoon extra-virgin olive oil

2 large onions, sliced

FOR THE BÉCHAMEL

2 tablespoons unsalted butter

2 tablespoons all-purpose flour

2 cups (475 ml) whole milk

Coarse salt and freshly ground black pepper

Freshly grated nutmeg

2 egg yolks (whites reserved for another use)

TO FINISH

1 tablespoon unsalted butter

4 egg yolks (whites reserved for another use)

2 cups (200g) freshly grated Parmesan cheese

Heat the horno, or a home oven, to 475°F (250°C).

Put the potatoes in a pot, cover them with plenty of cold water, add salt, and bring to a boil over medium heat. Let them bubble gently for about 15 minutes, until they are very tender. Drain thoroughly in a colander and return to the pot. Add 2 tablespoons of the butter and mash to a purée. Season to taste with salt, pepper, and a very small pinch of nutmeg. Set aside.

Place the olive oil and the remaining 1 tablespoon butter in a skillet over medium heat. When the butter has melted, add the onions. Sauté them for about 5 minutes, stirring occasionally, until they are golden brown. Remove the skillet from the heat before the onions are completely soft.

To make the béchamel, melt the butter in a saucepan over medium-low heat. Stir in the flour, and cook the roux gently for 3 minutes, without letting it brown. Bring the milk to a boil in a separate saucepan, then whisk it into the roux and cook, stirring, for about 5 minutes, until you feel it thicken substantially. Season to taste with salt, pepper, and a tiny bit of nutmeg. Let cool slightly, then vigorously whisk in the egg yolks. Set aside.

To finish the dish, when the horno is very hot, generously butter a 9-inch (23 cm)

cast-iron skillet or gratin dish with the remaining 1 tablespoon butter and layer the onions on the bottom. Cover evenly with the potato purée. With the back of a soup spoon, make four wells in the potato purée down to the onion layer and carefully add one egg yolk to each. Cover with the béchamel sauce, taking care not to break the yolks. Cover the béchamel completely with the Parmesan. Place the gratin dish in the hottest part of the oven and cook for about 5 minutes, rotating the dish two or three times so that it browns evenly, until the cheese is melted, browned, and bubbling but the egg yolks are still soft. Using a large spoon, aim to scoop up one unbroken egg yolk with each serving, and serve immediately.

SWEET POTATOES

FROM OVER THE SEA

I had always thought that boniatos (sweet potatoes) were another gift from the Americas to the world, but was happy to learn that we now think they were brought to us by Polynesians who came across the vast emptiness of the Pacific in their long canoes. What brave voyagers they were! These sweet tubers were a weekly purchase in my boyhood home, I suppose because they are well suited to the Andean climate and the extreme weather of our high mountain farms. They are often an afterthought in culinary books, while recipes for white potatoes could fill whole volumes.

Why is that?

I think it may be due to the fact that regular potatoes are so accepting of other flavors—content to be supporting actors, never striving for the spotlight. The sweet potato, on the other hand, is . . . well . . . sweet. This is why I have never encountered a child who will refuse a sweet potato. It is a vegetable with a distinct personality, not a background player. Like the (usually) more savory white potato, though, sweet potatoes can be crisped, baked, or roasted in hot coals. Every time I come across a particularly assertive spice mix—from Mexico or North Africa or India or Bali—I can be confident that I have found a new partner that can sing in harmony with the sweetness of the boniato. And to my way of thinking, there is nothing more satisfying than a sublimely creamy sweet potato roasted in the embers of a campfire, its charred skin sliced open with a knife and its flesh baptized in butter.

SWEET POTATO RESCOLDO, TWO WAYS

Often, the less you do to an ingredient the better it tastes. On an autumn afternoon, put some boniatos in the embers, ashes, and coals of your campfire, then take a walk for an hour or two. Watch the geese winging overhead in great convoys. On your return, pluck a slow-roasted sweet potato from the ashes it has cooked in. Split it, serve with butter, and you will be satisfied. Add a few other ingredients, and you'll begin to see how a bit of inspiration and intuition will allow you to keep reinventing this simple recipe.

WITH BUTTER AND CRUSHED RED PEPPER FLAKES

Serves 4 as a side dish

4 equal-size sweet potatoes, scrubbed
4 tablespoons unsalted butter
Fleur de sel
Crushed red pepper flakes

Prepare a fire and let the charcoal burn down to a bed of embers, coals, and ashes for rescoldo. If cooking indoors, preheat the oven to 375°F (190°C).

Bury the sweet potatoes in the embers, coals, and ashes, making sure they are completely and evenly covered. Roast until they are tender all the way through. The cooking time will vary depending on the size of the sweet potatoes: after about 20 minutes, part the embers with long-handled tongs and try to pierce a sweet potato all the way through with a long bamboo skewer. It will probably meet with some resistance toward the center and feel about half baked. Turn the potatoes over with the tongs and replace the embers and ashes, adjusting them as necessary for even cooking, and roast for about 20 minutes longer. When the sweet potatoes are done, carefully dig them out and wipe off the ashes with a dish towel or paper towels.

continued

If cooking indoors, arrange the sweet potatoes on a sheet pan and roast for about 45 minutes, or until tender all the way through.

To serve, split the sweet potatoes open, add a tablespoon of butter to each, and season to taste with fleur de sel and red pepper flakes.

WITH YOGURT AND MINT-ALMOND GREMOLATA

PICTURED ON PAGE 52

Much of my culinary philosophy is woven into this recipe. The cool creaminess of yogurt contrasted with the warm creaminess of the potato. The crunch of the almonds against the smoothness of the boniato. Honey to play on its inherent sweetness, with lemon as a counterpoint. Herbs because they provide top notes that sing out like piccolos in an orchestra. Olive oil because it always lifts flavor. Salt and pepper because they improve everything.

Serves 6 as a side dish, 3 as a main course

3 large sweet potatoes, scrubbed

A handful of fresh parsley leaves, chopped

¼ cup chopped fresh mint leaves

⅓ cup (35 g) chopped toasted almonds or walnuts

½ cup (118 ml) extra-virgin olive oil, plus more for drizzling

¼ teaspoon honey

Grated zest of 1 lemon

Coarse salt and freshly ground black pepper

Fleur de sel

1 cup (237 ml) plain yogurt, chilled

Roast the sweet potatoes as described above.

While the sweet potatoes are roasting, make the gremolata. Whisk together the parsley, mint, almonds, olive oil, honey, and lemon zest in a small bowl. Season to taste with salt and pepper. Set aside.

When the sweet potatoes are done, cool them very slightly, then cut them crosswise in half. With your fingers protected by a dish towel, slowly push the skin inward so the insides explode up from the top. Transfer the sweet potatoes to serving plates. Sprinkle with fleur de sel to taste, drizzle with olive oil, and add a large spoonful of cold yogurt to each potato. Spoon some gremolata over the yogurt and serve the rest on the side.

SWEET POTATO CHIPS
WITH PARSLEY AND GARLIC

Eat one, and you will be convinced. These chips are perfect just as they are, but are also sturdy enough to serve as vehicles for guacamole.

Serves 6

3 medium sweet potatoes, scrubbed

About 4 cups (1 L) oil (preferably a combination of olive and vegetable oils), for deep-frying

3 garlic cloves, minced

A large handful of fresh parsley leaves, finely chopped

Fleur de sel

Prepare a fire for medium-high heat and set a grate over it. Pull out a large deep cast-iron pot, such as a caldero or Dutch oven.

Slice the sweet potatoes very thinly on a mandoline and pat them dry.

Pour the oil into the caldero or deep cast-iron pot—it should be no more than half full. Warm the oil on the grate or on the stovetop over medium-high heat until a thermometer reads 350°F (180°C), or until the oil hisses and bubbles around a bit of potato when you drop it in. Line one or more sheet pans with paper towels and have them ready to drain the cooked potatoes.

Add a handful of sweet potatoes and fry for 1 to 2 minutes, until the chips are evenly golden and crispy. Use a long-handled spider or skimmer to separate them, if necessary. Adjust the heat as needed to keep the oil around 350°F (180°C). Scoop the chips out onto the prepared sheet pans to drain as they are done. Repeat

with the remaining potatoes, keeping the oil hot enough to fry the chips but taking care not to burn them. While the chips are still hot, season them with the garlic, parsley, and fleur de sel and serve immediately.

TORTILLA ESPAÑOLA DE BONIATOS

Every culture has its primal comfort food, and every family insists that the way their grandmother made it is the *only* way to prepare it, and any deviation brands transgressors as heretics. So here is my little heresy: I make this Spanish classic with sweet potatoes rather than white potatoes. In every other way it is just like the tortilla española that is a universally beloved tapa at every bar in Spain. One piece of advice: Have courage and believe in yourself when it comes time to flip the not-quite-done tortilla onto a plate and slide it back into the pan. If you are valiant in this, you will triumph!

Serves 4

1½ pounds (680 g) sweet potatoes, peeled
1 cup (237 ml) extra-virgin olive oil, plus more if needed
1 medium onion, roughly chopped
9 large eggs
Coarse salt

Prepare a fire for medium-low heat and set a grate over it. Pull out a 10-inch (25 cm) cast-iron skillet. If cooking indoors, you can use either a 10-inch (25 cm) cast-iron or nonstick skillet over medium-low heat.

Quarter the sweet potatoes lengthwise and slice them very thinly.

Warm the olive oil in the skillet. Add the potatoes, then the onion, and keep the heat low enough so the oil gently bubbles. The goal is to cook the potatoes and onion until they are tender, without browning them. Cover the skillet and cook for 3 minutes. Remove the lid and gently jiggle the pan to toss and turn the potatoes and onion. If they are browning, reduce the heat further. Replace the lid and cook for another 4 minutes. Check on the potatoes by removing one slice, blowing on it to cool, then tasting for doneness. It should be tender. I find that the potatoes usually need another 2 to 4 minutes. When the potatoes and onion are nicely cooked, drain them in a sieve set over a bowl and cool for about 10 minutes. Save the oil. It's still perfect for cooking.

Beat the eggs in a bowl with a pinch of salt. When the potatoes and onion are warm—not hot—to the touch, stir them into the eggs to combine. Pour the mixture into the skillet and set it over very low heat. Cook gently, jiggling and tilting the pan to allow the uncooked eggs to move freely, until the eggs are set and golden on the bottom. Occasionally run a spatula all around the edges to pull the cooked mixture away from the sides of the skillet. This will keep the tortilla from sticking when you unmold it.

Now comes the moment of truth when you must be fearless! When the eggs are almost set, run the spatula all around the sides of the skillet again to loosen the tortilla, then remove the pan from the heat. Cover the skillet with a large flat plate. Using oven mitts or pot holders, hold the plate with one hand and the skillet in the other and in one quick motion turn the skillet upside down to invert the tortilla onto the plate, cooked side up. Add more olive oil to the skillet, return it to the heat, and carefully slide the tortilla back into it, still cooked side up, then cook for 2 to 4 minutes. Now take the skillet in one hand, jiggle it again to loosen the bottom, and slide the tortilla onto a serving plate. Let it rest there for a few minutes to gather its wits. Cut it like a pie and serve.

TOMATOES

TOMATO TIME IN TUSCANY

Although I worked in many of the most glamorous restaurants in Europe when I was in my teens and early twenties, I didn't fully appreciate tomatoes until I took a job in a much less grandiose restaurant—Trattoria Maiano, in the Tuscan hill town of Fiesole just outside Florence.

The proprietor, Aldo Landi, and his wife lived upstairs from the restaurant. One afternoon, during a lull in the kitchen, he invited me up for a grand tour of the family quarters.

"This is my wife's room," Signor Landi said. "And this one is mine." There were two beds in his room. One for him and one for his dog, he explained. Most extraordinarily, hanging above his bed were eighteen hams!

In the controlled chaos of his kitchen, I noted how he would slice into a tomato and pull it apart with his fingers so that it looked anything but neat. The phrase that leaps to mind is "slightly destroyed." Then he'd dress the tomato simply with oil, vinegar, salt, and pepper: so perfect! Often those tomatoes were plump and soft, very ripe. When they reach that state, there is great concentration of flavor.

Whether I serve it raw or cooked, concentrating the natural flavor of a ripe tomato is always my goal. Tomatoes are especially suited for the plancha, where they will develop a beautiful charred crust, just like a perfectly cooked steak. Or dress them with olive oil before cooking for deep flavor without the burning. Both are equally good, in my mind. Or confit them ever so slowly in even more olive oil and they become soft, smooth, and sweet: the taste of summer on a plate.

TOMATO CONFIT

This is a very simple recipe, but because it is so simple, it is important that you use the best ingredients. Choose ripe beefsteak or heirloom tomatoes; their round shape and bulk are amply meaty. I prefer good olive oil to a neutral oil for its floral notes. Your goal is tomatoes that hold their shape and are tender and creamy. As the tomatoes cook, the liquid should gently simmer. Check your tomatoes from time to time just as you would look in on a sleeping infant. Serve the tomatoes as a side dish or stuff with cheese (see page 66). Crush into a sauce or use as a building block for other recipes, such as Pan Chato with Fennel (page 212).

Serves 6

1 cup (237 ml) extra-virgin olive oil, plus more if needed

6 equal-size ripe, meaty tomatoes (about 8 ounces/230 g each), preferably beefsteak or heirloom, cored

1 large head of garlic, cloves separated and peeled

1 large red onion, cut into small pieces

A handful of fresh herbs, such as thyme sprigs, sage leaves, oregano leaves

2 teaspoons red wine vinegar, plus more if needed

Coarse salt and freshly ground black pepper

Heat the horno, or a home oven, to 325°F (170°C).

Pour about a third of the oil into a baking dish that will snugly hold your tomatoes and is at least 2 inches (5 cm) deep. Set the tomatoes in the pan, cut side up, and stuff with the garlic cloves, onion, and herbs, tucking any excess around the tomatoes wherever you can. Sprinkle with the vinegar and add enough oil to come about halfway up the sides of the tomatoes. Season to taste with salt and pepper.

Bake, uncovered, for about 2 hours, until the tomatoes are very tender but still retain their shape. In the first half hour or so, they will throw off a lot of liquid, which will eventually reduce, allowing you to add more oil. Check the dish every 30 minutes or so and adjust the heat so the liquid maintains a gentle bubble. To brown the top, move the dish to the hottest part of the oven for the last few minutes; if cooking indoors, increase the temperature to 425°F (220°C) or run the dish under the broiler.

Let cool, then serve, or transfer the entire contents of the baking dish to an airtight container and store in the fridge for up to 5 days.

TOMATO CONFIT
WITH PEPATO CHEESE FILLING

Highly contrasting tastes and textures often play harmoniously together. Here the tomatoes are soft, quite sweet, and pleasantly acidic. Pepato is a semi-hard sheep's-milk pecorino, studded with whole black peppercorns. It is salty, with a peppery kick and a hint of caramel sweetness that wake up your palate.

Serves 4

4 Tomatoes Confit (page 65)

8 ounces (227 g) pecorino pepato cheese, shaved

Extra-virgin olive oil

Prepare a fire for medium heat and warm the plancha. If cooking indoors, heat a large cast-iron griddle over medium heat.

Place the tomatoes on a sheet pan and stuff a generous amount of cheese into the center of each. Drizzle the cheese with a little olive oil.

Brush the hot plancha or griddle generously with olive oil. Working with one tomato at a time and using a wide sharp-edged spatula, in one quick motion invert each tomato, cheese side down, onto the hot surface. Leave them there for several minutes, until the cheese has melted and each tomato is nicely browned. Lift the tomatoes off the plancha or griddle and flip them, cheese side up, onto a serving platter. Serve immediately.

TOMATO CONFIT SOUP

Sometimes—in fact, quite often—one good recipe can give birth to another. Case in point: this supremely satisfying soup based on confited tomatoes. Instead of discarding the garlic, onion, olive oil, and herbs, capture all the long-cooked savoriness they develop in those hours in the oven by puréeing them with the tomatoes. Garnish with fresh cilantro and enrich with bits of goat cheese before serving.

Serves 4

4 to 6 Tomatoes Confit (page 65), including the onion, garlic, and liquid from the confit mixture (remove and discard the herb stems)

Extra-virgin olive oil

Coarse salt and freshly ground black pepper

4 ounces (113 g) fresh goat cheese, crumbled

A few cilantro sprigs, chopped

Combine the tomatoes, onion, and garlic in a blender and blend until smooth, gradually adding the remaining liquid from the confit mixture until the taste and texture are to your liking. If it seems a little sharp from the vinegar, add more olive oil. Season to taste with salt and pepper.

To serve, heat the soup in a medium pot over low heat, then pour into individual bowls. Add a spoonful of goat cheese to each. Top with cilantro.

CHARRED TOMATOES
WITH GARLIC AND THYME

A lightly burnt tomato salad highlights the encounter of cooked and raw. The tomatoes are halved; scored; covered with thinly sliced garlic, onion, and thyme (or oregano, if that's what you have on hand); and lightly charred on the cut side. I like to eat this for lunch or as a light supper, served with an egg with crispy edges from a quick fry in olive oil, some griddled bread, and a glass of rosé.

Serves 4

4 ripe but firm round tomatoes

1 small red onion, halved and thinly sliced

4 garlic cloves, very thinly sliced

1 tablespoon fresh thyme leaves or chopped fresh oregano leaves

½ cup (118 ml) extra-virgin olive oil, plus more if needed

4 thick slices sourdough bread

4 eggs

Prepare a fire for high heat and warm the plancha. If cooking indoors, heat a large cast-iron griddle or skillet over high heat.

Halve the tomatoes crosswise and cut a shallow grid into the cut surfaces. Separate the onion slices into half rings. Press the garlic, thyme leaves, and onion firmly into the tomato grid to help them adhere when you invert them onto the grill.

Brush the hot plancha or griddle with some of the olive oil. When the oil shimmers, place a tomato, cut side up, on the palm of your hand, then flip it over onto the hot surface. Use a spatula to press it down so you don't burn yourself. Add the remaining tomatoes in the same manner. Cook the tomatoes until the garlic and onion slices are browned, 2 to 3 minutes, then transfer them cut side up to a serving platter. Drizzle with olive oil.

Meanwhile, brush the bread on both sides with olive oil. Generously oil another hot area of the plancha (or a separate large skillet, if cooking indoors) and toast the bread for a minute or two on each side. Transfer to serving plates. Add more oil to the plancha or skillet and fry the eggs until the edges are crisp and the yolks are done to your liking. Serve immediately.

BURNT TOMATO AND PLUM CAPRESE

Here's my variation on the caprese salad served everywhere in Italy. The classic recipe calls for raw tomato slices, but charring the tomato in wedges produces a gradation of texture—from burnt to ripe and sweet. While the tomatoes are equal parts acidity and sweetness, the plums are mostly sweet with a touch of acidity. Adding the crispy garlic chips brings some nuttiness into play without the garlicky sharpness.

Serves 4

4 ripe tomatoes, cut into large wedges

4 ripe plums, halved and pitted

¼ cup extra-virgin olive oil, plus more if needed

Coarse salt

8 ounces (227 g) bocconcini
(bite-size mozzarella balls)

Crispy Garlic Chips (page 296)

A handful of fresh basil leaves

Red wine vinegar

Prepare a fire for high heat and warm the plancha. If cooking indoors, heat one or more large cast-iron griddles or skillets over high heat.

Brush the cut sides of the tomatoes and plums with some of the olive oil and sprinkle with salt. Coat the hot plancha or griddle with olive oil. When the oil shimmers, place the tomatoes, cut side down, on the hot surface. Cook the tomatoes without moving them for about 2 minutes, until they are lightly charred on the cut side but still firm on top. With a sharp-edged spatula, lift the tomatoes off the plancha or griddle and invert them onto a wide serving platter. Repeat with the halved plums, browning them cut side down and adding them to the platter with the tomatoes.

To serve, scatter the bocconcini, garlic chips, and basil leaves over the top. Drizzle with more oil and with vinegar to taste.

BURNT CHERRY TOMATOES WITH SCALLIONS

The only thing you need to produce a happy outcome here is a little patience and very sweet cherry tomatoes. Once you put them on a hot plancha, *do not move them*! This allows the little tomatoes to develop an exquisite, charred crust. If you move them, all of their liquid will flow out, leaving you with tomatoes like deflated balloons. Delicious as they are on their own, these tomatoes instantly elevate a simple pasta with garlic and olive oil, avocado toast, or soft sheep's-milk cheese canapés.

Serves 4

1 pound (454 g) cherry tomatoes

Coarse salt

Extra-virgin olive oil

1 bunch scallions, green parts very thinly sliced (whites reserved for another use)

Fleur de sel

Prepare a fire for high heat and warm the plancha. If cooking indoors, heat a large cast-iron griddle over high heat.

Cut the tomatoes in half with a sharp serrated knife, place them in a bowl, and sprinkle with salt. Drizzle with olive oil and toss to coat. Carefully arrange the tomatoes on the very hot plancha or griddle cut side down and spaced well apart. Cook without disturbing the tomatoes for about 2 minutes, until you see a thin black line of char forming around the bottom but the tops remain firm. When they are done, the tomatoes will release easily from the hot surface. Use a sharp-edged spatula to transfer them cut side up to a serving platter.

Arrange the tomatoes on the platter and scatter the scallions over the top. Drizzle with olive oil, sprinkle with fleur de sel, and serve.

HEIRLOOM TOMATO SALAD WITH TORN BURRATA, TAPENADE, AND PINE NUTS

The less you do to cook or manipulate ingredients, the more critical it becomes to use them when they are at their peak of flavor, so make this salad only with vine-ripened tomatoes. At no other time will they achieve the mystical union of sweetness and acid that makes them irresistible. Roughly torn burrata with a nice soft chew in parts and overall luscious creaminess plays off the robust flavor of the tapenade, the crunch of pine nuts and breadcrumbs, and the full, rich flavor of the tomatoes.

Note: Chopping the olives by hand for the tapenade makes for a coarse and interesting texture. Extra tapenade can be stored in the refrigerator for up to 1 week.

Serves 6

FOR THE TAPENADE

1 cup (155 g) pitted kalamata olives, chopped

2 tablespoons capers, rinsed, dried, and chopped

1 teaspoon grated lemon zest

1 tablespoon fresh lemon juice

1½ teaspoons chopped fresh thyme leaves

½ cup (118 ml) extra-virgin olive oil

Freshly ground black pepper

FOR THE SALAD

6 ripe heirloom tomatoes, one kind or a variety

1¼ pounds (600 g) burrata cheese, at room temperature

Crunchy Breadcrumbs (page 287)

¼ cup pine nuts, toasted

Extra-virgin olive oil

First, make the tapenade. Combine the olives, capers, lemon zest, lemon juice, and thyme in a small bowl. Gradually whisk in the olive oil and season to taste with pepper.

To make the salad, slice the tomatoes into thick rounds and arrange them on a serving platter. Spoon about ¼ cup of the tapenade over the tomatoes. With two hands, tear the burrata apart over the center of the platter and set the pieces down, torn side up. Sprinkle with the breadcrumbs and pine nuts, drizzle with olive oil, and serve.

EGGPLANT

A DEBT OF FRIENDSHIP

I did not grow up eating eggplant. They are not particularly suited to the cool mountain climate and short growing season of Patagonia. My first serious encounter with them came when I was eighteen years old. I was living in Paris at the time, with barely enough money to afford a tiny room but determined to unlock the secrets of haute cuisine in the great restaurants of Europe. I had not yet made much progress on that ambition when Jimmy Vale, a friend with whom I used to ski back in the Andes, showed up and suggested a trip.

"Jimmy, you are very nice to invite me, but I don't have a cent," I said.

"Don't worry about the money," Jimmy said. "I've just come into an inheritance. You can pay me back someday."

When good fortune comes knocking at your door, I have found that it is always rewarding to walk on through, so off we went, and my Parisian ambitions were, for the moment, put aside. Our journey took us skiing in the Alps, then on to Rome and finally to Greece, where we planned to spend a week. It was so beautiful, and life was so sweet on the island of Mykonos, that I stayed for six months! I ate roasted lamb, drank local wine, and swam—or so I imagined—in the wake of dolphins in the clear blue waters of the Aegean. Spending that time with a lovely girlfriend made the visit even sweeter. If you are young and in love, I cannot think of a better place to step off life's treadmill for a few moments.

You cannot be in Greece that long without coming into daily contact with eggplant. In one way or another, they always find a way to the table. Their creaminess, their smokiness, their ability to form friendships with other ingredients were a revelation to me, and I have cooked with them ever since.

PS: As for my debt to Jimmy, every time he broke a large-denomination bill, I noted it down. Ten years later, I had my own restaurant in Buenos Aires and was doing very well. I invited Jimmy to dinner one night and gratefully settled up our financial account. I will always be in his debt, though, for that carefree interlude in my youth.

RESCOLDO EGGPLANT WITH PARSLEY, CHILE, AND AIOLI

There has always been a precarious balance between burnt and incinerated in my recipes. This is a fine line to walk, but I am a devotee of pushing ingredients to this perilous point, because something magical happens when smoke, char, and fire meet. Nature must have had this in mind when she created eggplant. I particularly like to cook them until their skins are black and wrinkled and the smokiness of the burnt skin permeates the eggplant's soft flesh. Ember-cooked eggplant are as creamy as a carefully stirred custard, and they drink deeply of the flavors in this simple recipe.

Serves 4

4 medium globe or large Italian eggplants
A handful of fresh parsley leaves
Crushed red pepper flakes
Extra-virgin olive oil
Best-quality red wine vinegar
1 cup (237 ml) Aioli (page 294)

Prepare a fire and let the charcoal burn down to a bed of embers, coals, and ashes for rescoldo.

Bury the whole eggplants completely in the glowing embers, coals, and ashes. After 10 minutes, part the embers with long-handled tongs, turn the eggplants, and roast until blackened and charred all over, about 5 minutes longer. They should be very tender all the way through when pierced with a long bamboo skewer. Remove from the fire and brush off the ashes, leaving most of the charred skin.

If cooking indoors, roast the eggplants on a foil-lined sheet pan under a hot broiler or over gas burners, turning occasionally, until the skin is charred and blackened on all sides and the inside is very tender, about 15 minutes.

To serve, slice open each eggplant lengthwise and arrange on a platter. Scatter with the parsley leaves and red pepper flakes to taste, then drizzle lightly with olive oil and a few drops of vinegar. Serve the aioli alongside.

VARIATION

RESCOLDO EGGPLANT WITH FRESH TOMATO REDUCTION

PICTURED OPPOSITE

As anyone who has a garden knows, when eggplants are in season, there are a lot of them to deal with. Tomatoes are at their most plentiful at the same time. This recipe takes advantage of both bounties.

Roast the eggplants as described above. Split open and top with Fresh Tomato Reduction (page 295), fresh basil leaves, and shaved Grana Padano or Parmesan cheese.

EGGPLANT MILANESA

Once in a great while, a new dish is born, and on the very first taste I'll tell myself, "This is so delightful in every way, surely someone must have dreamed it up a long time ago." But this Eggplant Milanesa was invented by Diego Irrera, my chef de cuisine at The Vines, in the wine district of Mendoza. He roasts an eggplant until it collapses, then breads it like you would for a milanesa or schnitzel. Crispy on the outside yet as creamy as custard on the inside, this savory eggplant "cutlet" has quickly become the favorite vegetarian main course in all of my restaurants. I prefer thick, pear-shaped globe or Italian eggplants for this dish. They must be well roasted for a pleasing note of smokiness. Once the charred skin is removed, the eggplant should be at least an inch (2.5 cm) thick. It is very important that you use fresh breadcrumbs (homemade rather than store-bought); the milanesas cook slowly and gently with a crisp, buttery, lightly golden crust.

Note: For a vegan version, use olive oil instead of butter.

Serves 4 as a main course

4 medium globe or large Italian eggplants

3 eggs

½ cup (25 g) chopped fresh parsley leaves

¼ cup chopped fresh oregano leaves

Coarse salt and freshly ground black pepper

2 cups (216 g) fresh breadcrumbs, made from crustless country bread

3 large garlic cloves, very thinly sliced

½ cup (113 ml) Clarified Butter (page 298)

4 tablespoons cold unsalted butter, cut into small pieces

A couple of handfuls of fresh young greens, such as arugula or mesclun

½ small red onion, very thinly sliced

Extra-virgin olive oil

Lemon wedges, for serving

Prepare a fire and let the charcoal burn down to a bed of embers, coals, and ashes for rescoldo.

Bury the whole eggplants completely in the glowing embers. After 10 minutes, use long-handled tongs to part the embers and turn the eggplants. Replace the embers and roast until blackened and charred all over, 5 to 10 minutes longer. The eggplants should be tender all the way through when pierced with a long bamboo skewer. Remove from the fire and place in a paper bag or covered bowl to steam. When cool enough to handle, carefully scrape off the charred peel, leaving the stems attached to keep the eggplants whole. If cooking indoors, char the eggplants by placing them on a foil-lined baking sheet under a very hot broiler for 15 to 20 minutes, turning occasionally, until completely blackened and tender inside. Cover with more foil, seal the edges, and steam as above, then peel. Alternatively, hold them with long-handled tongs over a gas burner for about 15 minutes, until the skin is blackened on all sides.

Add more coals to the fire for a plancha over medium-low heat. If cooking indoors, heat one or more large cast-iron griddles over medium-low heat.

continued

Beat the eggs in a wide, shallow bowl. Add the parsley and oregano, then season to taste with salt and pepper.

One at a time, using the stem as a handle, carefully dunk the whole eggplants into the egg mixture and lay them out on a sheet pan, being careful not to break them. Gently flatten them with your hands until they are an even thickness, about an inch (2.5 cm) or more. Cover the eggplants generously with some of the breadcrumbs, patting the crumbs gently but firmly onto the surface.

Turn the eggplants over and scatter the garlic over the top, gently pressing the slices in. Cover generously with more breadcrumbs, and pat them on so the eggplants are completely encased in crumbs.

Melt 4 tablespoons of the clarified butter on the hot plancha or griddles. Add the eggplants, garlic side down and spaced well apart. Cook very slowly until the breadcrumbs are golden brown and crisp (check by lifting just an edge with a spatula), about 4 minutes. Add small pieces of the cold butter around the sides if the pan becomes dry. Turn and cook on the other side with the remaining clarified butter until golden brown and crisp, about 4 minutes longer. Drain on paper towels.

Toss the greens in a bowl with the sliced onion and a drizzle of olive oil. Season to taste with salt and pepper. Top each eggplant with some greens and serve with lemon wedges alongside for squeezing over the top.

RATATOUILLE TIAN AND CHURRASCO

I have been bewitched by ratatouille ever since I was a young cook working in the famed kitchen of Roger Vergé. His restaurant, Moulin de Mougins, on the French Riviera, gave birth to a light style of cooking known as Cuisine of the Sun. The heavy sauces, butter, and cream of classic French cookery were eclipsed by recipes that Chef Roger created to highlight vegetables in season and the bright flavors of herbs, spices, and the citrus fruits of the South of France. Here are two homages to the traditional ratatouille.

A **tian** is the name of both a southern French earthenware baking dish and what's cooked in it—in this case, tightly packed rows of thinly sliced eggplant, tomato, and zucchini, baked slowly and gently in lots of olive oil. The vegetables are sliced into disks and stacked as they are cut, then trimmed flat on one rounded edge so they stand up on their sides in long rows in the baking dish. Don't worry if your disks are not of equal diameter—you can patch as necessary. The result is a creamy mélange on the inside and a crunchy bite on the outside. Remember: While your tian takes its time to bake slowly, the good in cooking, as in life, often comes with waiting. For the churrasco, the vegetables are sliced the same way but arranged in a flatter overlapping spiral pattern and baked very slowly until creamy inside but very crisp on the outside.

A **churrasco**, in Argentina, usually refers to a slice of beef quickly cooked. Even though my "ratatouille churrasco" is baked for two hours, the result, like a meat churrasco, is crisp on top but as succulent and satisfying as the classic. If you bake a tian and have leftovers, you can arrange them in a spiral on a sheet pan and reheat until crisp in a hot oven or under the broiler.

Serves 6

About 1¼ cups (250 ml) extra-virgin olive oil, plus more for drizzling

5 garlic cloves, peeled

About 2 pounds (1 kg) Italian eggplants or elongated globe eggplants

About 2 pounds (1 kg) thick zucchini or yellow squash

About 2 pounds (1 kg) ripe but firm tomatoes, such as plum tomatoes

Coarse salt and freshly ground black pepper

A small bunch of thyme

Crunchy Breadcrumbs (page 297; optional)

Heat the horno, or a home oven, to 325°F (170°C).

Pour the olive oil into a small bowl and grate the garlic into it with a Microplane. Stir well and set aside.

Slice the eggplants, zucchini, and tomatoes as thinly as possible, preferably on a mandoline, holding them in three separate bowls. If the tomato is very ripe, you will probably need to slice it by hand.

To make a tian: Generously coat the bottom of an 8 by 10 by 2-inch (20 by 25 by 5 cm) baking dish (or a clay tian) with the garlic oil.

Start making little stacks of alternating vegetables on a cutting board. Set a stack on its side and slice off just enough of one rounded edge so the stack will stand upright on its cut side, then transfer it to the baking dish. Repeat with the remaining stacks, filling the baking dish with long rows of vegetables, packing them in as tightly together as possible (this keeps them

You want to keep the level of oil/liquid about halfway up the side of the dish.

For the last 30 minutes, move the tian closer to the fire to increase the heat for browning. If cooking indoors, increase the oven temperature to 450°F (230°C). The top edges should become very brown and crusty. Serve sprinkled with the remaining thyme and crunchy breadcrumbs, if desired.

To make churrascos: Generously coat the bottom of 2 sheet pans with a few tablespoons of the garlic oil, leaving the garlic behind.

Stack alternating disks of vegetables on a cutting board, then fan them out in the palm of your hand (like playing cards) and arrange them into six overlapping spirals, like pinwheels, on the prepared pans. Sprinkle with most of the thyme leaves, generously cover with the garlic oil (including the garlic), and bake for about 2 hours, until tender and creamy in the center. Baste with more garlic oil as needed. For the last 30 minutes, increase the heat by moving the churrascos closer to the fire until they become very brown and crunchy, rotating them now and then to prevent burning. If cooking indoors, increase the oven temperature to 450°F (230°C) or run the churrascos briefly under the broiler.

Using a large wide spatula, transfer the churrascos to serving plates. Top with the remaining thyme and crunchy breadcrumbs, if desired, and serve immediately. Or, to serve family-style, stack two or three cooked churrascos on top of each other like a layer cake with crunchy breadcrumbs and herbs in between. Cut into wedges for serving.

juicy while baking). Season to taste with salt and pepper, then pour the over the vegetables, leaving about ½ inch (1.25 cm) of clearance at the top. Tuck in the sprigs of thyme here and there, reserving 2 for garnish.

Set the tian on a sheet pan (in case it bubbles over) and bake for about 3 hours, until very tender and creamy. Every half hour or so, check the amount of liquid and rotate the tian. The vegetables will release a lot of liquid at first, and you don't want it to bubble over the baking dish.

EGGPLANT A LA PLANCHA, FOUR WAYS

Eggplant slices are easy to cook on the plancha. And because eggplant accepts other flavors so easily, the only limit on ways to serve it is the cook's imagination (and the availability of ingredients). To do eggplants justice, your goal is a soft and smooth inside and a golden brown crispness on the surface. There is only one way to achieve this . . . *cook slowly over low heat*! You don't want the outside to get browned before the inside is cooked through.

Serve dressed simply with fresh herbs and a squeeze of lemon, or turn the eggplants into a more substantial dish by topping with any of the suggestions that follow.

Serves 4

2 medium globe eggplants

½ cup (118 ml) extra-virgin olive oil, plus more if needed

A handful of soft, fresh herbs, roughly torn

Lemon wedges

Fleur de sel

Prepare a fire for low heat and warm the plancha. If cooking indoors, heat one or more large cast-iron griddles over low heat.

Cut off the stems, then slice the eggplants lengthwise about ½ inch (1.25 cm) thick. Pat dry with paper towels. With a sharp knife, lightly score all the cut sides. Brush one side generously with olive oil.

Brush the hot plancha or griddle with some of the olive oil. When the oil shimmers, add the eggplant slices, oiled side down, without crowding. Cook until nicely browned on the bottom, about 6 minutes. Brush the other side generously with oil and turn, adding more oil if necessary to the pan at any time if it seems dry. Cook the other side until the eggplant is crisp, browned, and very tender when pierced with a fork, about 6 minutes longer. Arrange the slices on a platter, then scatter the herbs over the top. Drizzle with oil and serve with the lemon wedges alongside. Sprinkle with fleur de sel and serve.

VARIATIONS

EGGPLANT WITH YOGURT, SOY, PISTACHIOS, AND MINT

PICTURED OPPOSITE

On the island of Mykonos, the combination of eggplant, yogurt, and mint is served everywhere. Basting with soy sauce is something I added for a salty, pungent finish on the surface of each eggplant slice. It's best to serve this dish when the eggplant is piping hot and the yogurt is quite cold. The contrast wakes up the palate most pleasantly.

Serves 4

continued

1 cup (227 ml) plain yogurt, chilled

12 drops Tabasco sauce

About ½ cup (118 ml) soy sauce

A large handful of fresh mint leaves, torn

¼ cup toasted pistachios, roughly chopped

Combine the yogurt and Tabasco to taste in a small bowl; mix well. Grill the eggplant slices as described on page 89, then coat both sides with the soy sauce, and top with the seasoned yogurt, mint, and pistachios. Serve the remaining yogurt on the side.

EGGPLANT WITH CUCUMBER, SHALLOT, ALMONDS, AND CILANTRO

PICTURED OPPOSITE

Here we have a trio of textures. Cucumber is crisp. Almonds are crunchy. Eggplant is smooth. I love how they collide. And cilantro . . . well, it's always a statement; some people love her and some run away. I adore her. The tastes and textures in this little dressing clash while the eggplant receives all in a state of Zen accommodation.

Serves 4

1 medium cucumber, peeled, seeded, and finely diced

3 tablespoons finely diced shallot

3 tablespoons roughly chopped toasted almonds

A small handful of fresh cilantro leaves, chopped

¼ cup extra-virgin olive oil

2 teaspoons red wine vinegar, plus more if needed

Coarse salt and freshly ground black pepper

Combine the cucumber, shallot, almonds, cilantro, olive oil, and vinegar in a bowl. Mix well and season to taste with salt and pepper and with more vinegar, if desired. Grill the eggplant slices as described on page 89, then spoon the dressing over the sliced eggplant.

EGGPLANT WITH FRESH TOMATO REDUCTION, BASIL, AND CHEESE

If you find yourself with a surplus of overripe tomatoes, as I often do, make an easy fresh tomato reduction and have it on hand for a light sauce like this, or whatever excites your appetite. It is supernal.

Serves 4

1 cup (237 ml) Fresh Tomato Reduction (page 295)

7 ounces (200 g) Grana Padano or Parmesan cheese, shaved

A fistful of fresh basil leaves, roughly torn

Extra-virgin olive oil

Freshly ground black pepper

Fleur de sel

Grill the eggplant slices as described on page 89 and arrange them on a large platter. Spoon the tomato reduction over the cooked eggplant slices, then top with the cheese and basil. Drizzle with olive oil and season to taste with pepper and fleur de sel.

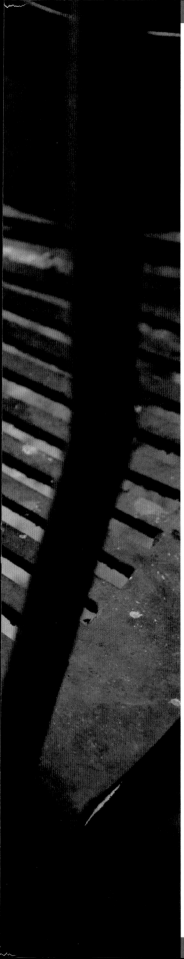

ARTICHOKES

THE JOKE WAS ON ME

By a stroke of fortune, my early restaurant ventures in South America earned me just enough money in our peak holiday season that I was able to offer my labor for free to the reigning masters of cuisine in France and Italy. The passions of youth are not to be denied, and mine was to learn the secrets of haute cuisine. I wrote to all the Michelin three-star restaurants in France. Finally, one decided to take me up on my offer: Ledoyen, an elegant Parisian restaurant under chef Francis Trocellier.

I quickly found that learning the art of haute cuisine takes a bit more effort than sitting in a yoga pose at the foot of the master and absorbing his wisdom (back in those days, it was always "his wisdom," never "hers"). Instead, it was a matter of endless repetition of menial tasks until you could do them in your sleep. Among the least-favorite tasks in the kitchen was prepping artichokes. Peeling them and cutting away the pesky fur inside without mutilating the precious artichoke heart is an art that you learn when you set about trimming your ten thousandth artichoke.

My apprenticeship started when Monsieur Trocellier tasked me with peeling cases of artichokes stacked six feet (2 m) high. Working swiftly and precisely, he demonstrated how to do it, then left me with a few hundred artichokes. If you have ever peeled an artichoke, you know that it takes great concentration, so much so that it wasn't until some time had passed that I realized the whole kitchen brigade was laughing at me.

What had I done to cause this outbreak of laughter? It seemed that they were all pointing at something under the table. I was puzzled and then I looked down. I had been so intent on peeling artichokes that I hadn't noticed that someone had sneaked under the table and painted my shoes white!

Apparently, this was the way all kitchen apprentices were welcomed to the Ledoyen team.

In the years since, I have recovered from this embarrassing introduction to artichokes and learned that from leaf to heart to stem, artichokes can be braised, roasted, or grilled over a wood fire, and play the role of loving but never overbearing companion to herbs, spices, and fresh vegetables.

ARTICHOKES MIMOSA WITH AIOLI

When mimosa trees are in bloom, they are festooned with small flowers of yellow and white; they dot the landscape in Provence. The colors make them look quite similar to a boiled egg roughly mashed with a fork: hence the name. Eggs done this way are divine on artichokes and pretty great on asparagus, too. Enrobed in slightly tart, slightly pungent aioli, these artichokes will reveal layer upon layer of texture and flavor as you savor them.

Serves 4

Coarse salt

8 medium globe artichokes, preferably long-stemmed

2 lemons, halved

4 eggs

Red wine vinegar

¼ cup finely chopped fresh parsley leaves

½ cup (118 g) Aioli (page 293)

Fleur de sel

Prepare a fire for high heat and set a grate over it. Pull out a pot large enough to hold all the artichokes, such as a caldero or Dutch oven (or a stockpot if cooking indoors). Fill the pot about halfway with water, and season with salt. Set the pot on the grate (or on the stovetop over high heat) and bring to a boil.

Keeping the stems attached, pull off the toughest outer leaves of the artichokes. Lay them down on their sides and, with a sharp serrated knife (bread knife), slice the spiky top half straight off, then snip off any remaining spiky tips with kitchen shears. Pare off the tough skin around the bottoms and stems, rubbing the cut areas with lemon juice as you go.

Add the artichokes and squeezed lemons to the boiling water, partially cover the pot, and cook over medium heat for about 15 minutes, depending on the artichokes' size, until they are tender all the way through when pierced with a skewer. Drain the artichokes thoroughly in a colander, stems pointing up. Discard the lemons.

Meanwhile, fill a saucepan with enough water to cover the eggs and bring to a boil over medium heat. Lower the eggs into the water and boil for 6 minutes. While the eggs are cooking, fill a bowl with ice and water. With a wide spider or skimmer, transfer the eggs directly into the ice water to stop the cooking. Crack the shells and peel the eggs, put them in a bowl, and mash roughly with a fork. Set aside.

Carefully cut the artichokes in half lengthwise all the way through the stem. Lay them down on a flat surface and scrape out the fuzzy inedible chokes with a teaspoon. As they are done, arrange them cut side up on a wide platter.

Season the mashed egg to taste with a few drops of vinegar, add the parsley, and stir in the aioli. Spoon the mixture over the artichoke hearts, season with fleur de sel, and serve.

ARTICHOKES A LA PLANCHA WITH LEMON CONFIT AND TOASTED ALMONDS

Artichokes take a while to cook through at a low boil, but once you've done that, they brown up beautifully on the plancha. It is often said that artichokes don't pair well with wine. That is largely true, but for some reason, among the many mysteries of taste, champagne goes quite well with artichokes. Even though I am not much of a champagne drinker, I have been known to raise a glass when artichokes are on the menu.

Serves 4 to 6

Coarse salt

2 teaspoons fennel seeds

1 head of garlic, halved crosswise

2 bay leaves

1 teaspoon whole black peppercorns

6 large globe artichokes, with stems

2 lemons, halved

6 tablespoons extra-virgin olive oil, plus more as needed

½ cup (113 g) toasted almonds, roughly chopped

In a large pot, bring about 4 inches (10 cm) of salted water to a boil with the fennel seeds, garlic, bay leaves, and peppercorns.

While waiting for the water to boil, pull off the tough outside leaves of each artichoke and trim off the bottom tip of the stem. Lay the artichoke down on its side and, with a sharp serrated knife (bread knife), slice the spiky tops straight off about two-thirds of the way down to the base. Pare off the tough skin around the base and stem and rub all the cut areas with lemon juice.

Add the artichokes and squeezed lemon halves to the boiling water and adjust the heat to maintain a low boil. Partially cover the pot and cook for about 20 minutes, depending on the artichokes' size, until they are tender all the way through when pierced through the bottom with a skewer. Drain them thoroughly in a colander, stem side up, reserving the lemon halves, garlic cloves, fennel seeds, and peppercorns.

Cut the artichokes lengthwise in half and scrape out the fuzzy inedible chokes with a teaspoon. Pat them dry with paper towels. Place them in a bowl with 4 tablespoons of the olive oil and the reserved garlic and spices and toss lightly to coat. Set aside to marinate for up to 2 hours.

Tear the reserved lemon halves into quarters, then lay them skin side down on a flat surface. With a sharp paring knife, scrape away every bit

of white pith and pulp, leaving only the yellow zest. Cut the zest into 1-inch (2.5 cm) strips and place in a small bowl. Drizzle with the remaining 2 tablespoons olive oil, toss to coat, and set aside.

Meanwhile, prepare a fire for medium heat and warm the plancha (or heat a large cast-iron griddle over medium heat, if cooking indoors).

Brush the hot plancha or griddle with olive oil. When the oil shimmers, add the artichokes.

Brown the artichokes until crisp and golden on all sides, about 5 minutes. When they are almost done, add the lemon strips to the hot surface to lightly brown. Arrange on a serving platter, scatter the toasted almonds over the top, and serve.

ARTICHOKES, FAVAS, AND PEAS

This salad is full of the spirit of spring, marked by the return of green growing things. But because this dish is so simple, everything depends on the peas being sweet, the favas still small and tender, and the artichokes soft and delicate. Pay careful attention when cooking the peas; you want them just at the point of doneness. Mint pulls the dish together; this cooling green is among the first herbs of the season.

Serves 4

4 large globe artichokes

2 lemons: 1 halved, 1 cut into wedges for serving

Coarse salt

1 large bay leaf

3 tablespoons extra-virgin olive oil, plus more as needed

Freshly ground black pepper

2 cups (240 g) shelled, blanched, and peeled young fresh fava beans

1½ cups (180 g) shelled young fresh peas

Crunchy Breadcrumbs (page 297)

Leaves from a few mint sprigs, torn

Prepare a fire for medium heat and warm the plancha. (Or pull out a large cast-iron griddle if cooking indoors.)

Meanwhile, pull off the tough outside leaves of each artichoke and trim off the bottom tip of the stem. Lay the artichoke down on its side and, with a sharp serrated knife, slice the spiky tops straight off about two-thirds of the way down. Pare off the tough skin around the base and stem and rub all the cut areas with lemon juice.

Bring a large pot of salted water to a boil over high heat and add the artichokes, the squeezed lemon halves, and the bay leaf. Cook for about 20 minutes, until the artichokes are tender all the way through when pierced with a skewer. Drain thoroughly and let cool, reserving the lemon.

Tear the cooked lemon into pieces. Scrape away and discard every bit of white pith from the zest and set the zest aside.

Cut the artichokes in half and pull off all but the very tenderest remaining leaves. Using a teaspoon, scrape out and discard the fuzzy inedible chokes. Cut the trimmed halves in half again and set aside in a bowl. Drizzle with 2 tablespoons of the olive oil, toss to coat, and season to taste with salt and pepper.

Meanwhile, bring a saucepan of salted water to a rolling boil over high heat. Add the fava beans and cook for 2 to 4 minutes, until just tender. Drain in a colander under cold running water and set aside in a bowl. Separately, bring another saucepan of salted water to a boil and add the peas, but cook them only for about a minute, until they are tender. Immediately drain in a colander under cold running water. Add the peas to the favas and season to taste with a tablespoon or so of olive oil, salt, and pepper.

Brush the hot plancha with olive oil (if cooking indoors, heat the griddle over medium heat, then brush with oil) and add the artichokes. Brown the artichokes until nicely crisped, 3 to 4 minutes.

To serve, arrange the favas and peas on a wide serving platter with the browned artichokes and reserved lemon zest on top, and shower with crunchy breadcrumbs and torn mint leaves. Serve with lemon wedges on the side.

SMASHED ARTICHOKES AND CRISPY KALE

I like smashable foods. Just as with potatoes or beets, artichokes—when smashed and tossed on the plancha—will crisp and brown on the outside and turn crumbly within so you get two textures in one bite. Kale is also sturdy enough to crisp up, instead of surrendering limply to the heat like a less-hardy green. Combine the two and you have a savory mouthful, awakened by the sharpness of fresh chives.

Note: I will often make a simple meal of artichokes from the plancha served with a robust cheese—Tomme is divine, so is aged Manchego or a caramelly aged cheddar such as Cabot Clothbound.

Serves 4

4 large globe artichokes

3 lemons: 1 halved, 2 cut into wedges for serving

Coarse salt

1 bay leaf

6 tablespoons extra-virgin olive oil, plus more for the plancha

12 large curly kale leaves, tough stems removed

1 bunch chives, chopped

Fleur de sel

Prepare a fire for medium-high heat and warm the plancha. (Or pull out a large cast-iron griddle if cooking indoors.)

Meanwhile, trim the artichokes. Lay an artichoke down on its side and, with a sharp serrated knife (bread knife), slice off the spiky top about two-thirds of the way down to the base. Trim the stem and pare off the tough skin around the bottom, rubbing the cut areas with lemon juice as you go. Repeat with the remaining artichokes.

Bring a large pot of salted water to a boil and add the artichokes, the squeezed lemon halves, and the bay leaf. Partially cover the pot and cook for about 20 minutes, until the artichokes are tender all the way through when pierced with a skewer. Drain thoroughly in a colander until cool enough to handle.

Pull off all the tough leaves and cut the artichokes in half lengthwise. Using a teaspoon, scoop out and discard the fuzzy inedible chokes. Trim away any remaining tough bits with a sharp paring knife. Set an artichoke half cut side down on a flat surface and, using both hands, gently but firmly smash it as flat as you can. If it won't smash down flat, try it from another angle. It might look a bit messy, but that's okay. Scrape up the artichoke with a wide sharp-edged spatula and set aside on a sheet pan. Repeat with the remaining artichokes. When they are all smashed, drizzle them with 2 tablespoons of the olive oil and set aside.

Brush the heated plancha with oil (if cooking indoors, heat the griddle over medium-high heat, then brush with oil) and arrange the kale leaves on the hot surface. Let them soften for about 3 minutes, then drizzle 2 tablespoons of the olive oil over them and flip them to cook on the other side until crisp, about 2 minutes.

Meanwhile, brush a separate area of the plancha or a separate griddle with oil and transfer the smashed artichokes to it. Cook over medium heat to brown the bottoms, 2 to 3 minutes. Scrape up the artichokes with the spatula and turn them to lightly brown the other side. Lift them with the spatula and set them on top of the kale. Scatter the chives over the top and use the spatula to transfer to individual plates. Sprinkle with fleur de sel and serve with the lemon wedges alongside for squeezing over the top.

CRISPY ARTICHOKES WITH LABNEH AND LIMONETA

This preparation is similar to the deep-fried artichokes on page 108 but a little quicker to make and more manageable to eat with a fork or fingers. There are more surfaces to crisp up when cooking quartered artichokes than whole ones. And when it comes to cooking vegetables, there is no such thing as too much crust.

Labneh is denser than Greek yogurt, making it more like cream cheese. You can also try a smooth creamy goat cheese or sheep's-milk cheese.

Serves 4

4 large globe artichokes

2 lemons

1 cup (237 ml) extra-virgin olive oil, plus more if needed

Coarse salt and freshly ground black pepper

8 ounces (227 g) labneh or other creamy cheese

2 tablespoons minced fresh chives

To trim the artichokes, pull off all the tough outside leaves and trim off the bottom end of the stem. Lay the artichoke down on its side and, with a sharp serrated knife (bread knife), slice the spiky tops straight off about two-thirds down to the base. Pare off the tough skin around the base and stem and rub all the cut areas with the juice of 1 lemon.

Fill a large pot about halfway with water and bring to a boil. Add the artichokes and squeezed lemon halves and boil gently for about 15 minutes depending on the artichoke, until they are tender all the way through when pierced with a skewer. Drain in a colander until cool enough to handle. Cut them into thirds or quarters, depending on the size. Using a teaspoon, scrape out and discard the fuzzy inedible chokes. Trim off any other bits that look tough. Pat them dry and place in a bowl with about 3 tablespoons of the olive oil, or enough to coat them and keep them moist. The recipe may be made ahead to this point. If prepping ahead, the artichokes can be held in the bowl for up to 2 hours until you are ready to fry.

Prepare a fire for medium-high heat and set a grate over it. Pull out a large deep cast-iron pot, such as a caldero or Dutch oven.

To make the limoneta, grate the zest from the remaining lemon and set the zest aside. Cut the lemon in half and strain the juice into a small bowl. With a fork, gradually beat 3 to 4 tablespoons of olive oil into the lemon juice, tasting as you go, until the flavor is to your liking. Season to taste with salt and pepper and set aside.

Set the pot on the grate (or over medium-high heat, if cooking indoors) and add about 4 inches (10 cm) of oil. Line a sheet pan with paper towels and have ready a long-handled spider or skimmer. When the oil is hot enough to hiss and bubble around an artichoke leaf as a test, fry the quartered artichokes in batches. Turn them as they cook to crisp on all sides. After about 3 minutes, lift them out with the spider and transfer to the prepared sheet pan to drain.

To serve, spoon some of the labneh onto serving plates. Top with the artichokes and drizzle with the limoneta. Sprinkle with the reserved lemon zest and the chives. Serve immediately.

DEEP-FRIED WHOLE ARTICHOKES WITH TAHINI AND BLACK SESAME YOGURT

In Rome, the ancient Jewish community is famed for deep-frying artichokes until they look like giant blossoms preserved in amber at the moment that they are about to unfurl. Their color comes from the caramelizing effect of deep-frying in bubbling oil. I learned to love these when I worked at Enoteca Pinchiorri, a Michelin-starred restaurant in Florence. However, my affection for fried artichokes wasn't because we served them at the restaurant, but rather because they were offered in the surrounding food stalls at prices that a young kitchen apprentice could afford. The yogurt dressing is a cooling counterpoint, studded with the aromatic nuttiness of black sesame seeds. I am indebted to Sebastian Benitez, my chef at Los Fuegos in Miami, for this delicious dish.

Serves 2

2 lemons, halved

4 medium globe artichokes

Olive oil (or half olive oil, half vegetable oil), for deep-frying

Leaves from a few thyme sprigs

FOR THE YOGURT SAUCE

1½ cups (356 ml) plain Greek yogurt

2 tablespoons tahini

2 tablespoons fresh lemon juice

1 garlic clove, grated

2 teaspoons toasted black sesame seeds

Coarse salt

Prepare a fire for medium-high heat and set a grate over it. Pull out a large deep cast-iron pot, such as a caldero or Dutch oven.

Fill a large bowl halfway with water, squeeze the lemons into it, and add the squeezed halves. Trim the stems of the artichokes, leaving about an inch (2.5 cm) attached. Pull off the tough outer leaves and lay the artichokes down on a flat surface. With a sharp serrated knife (bread knife), slice the spiky top leaves straight off about two-thirds of the way down to the base. Then slice off the remaining leaves at a slight angle while rotating the artichoke to form a pinecone shape. Pare off the tough skin around the base and stem. Using a sharp-edged teaspoon or melon baller, scoop out and discard the fuzzy inedible chokes, then immediately submerge the artichokes in the lemon water.

To make the yogurt sauce, whisk together the yogurt, tahini, lemon juice, garlic, and 1 teaspoon of the sesame seeds in a bowl. When thoroughly blended, whisk in salt to taste. Set aside. (The yogurt sauce can be made ahead of time and chilled.)

Line a sheet pan with paper towels and have ready a long-handled spider or skimmer.

Set the caldero or pot on the grate (or over medium-high heat, if cooking indoors) and add olive oil to come about halfway up the sides. Heat the oil to about 325°F (170°C). The oil should bubble gently around an artichoke leaf dropped in as a test.

Add the artichokes in batches and fry them slowly, turning them occasionally as

they brown, for about 15 minutes. When they are golden brown and very crisp, lift them out with the spider and transfer to the prepared sheet pan, placing them cut side down to drain.

Spoon the yogurt sauce onto serving plates, and arrange 2 artichokes on each. Sprinkle with the remaining sesame seeds and the thyme leaves, and serve immediately.

Ah, Flowers!

The story goes like this:

I remember a scene from my childhood as if it were today. Full of color and life: the garden of Alfred and Ruth von Ellrichshausen. They had escaped Germany during World War II and settled in our town, Bariloche. I can still picture Alfred working in their nursery full of blooming roses, lilies, carnations, camellias—more flowers than I could name when I first encountered them at age six. Just like an English gentleman, Alfred always wore a tie when he worked in the garden. Did the flowers know they were being so formally attended?

I have a particularly vivid memory of Sunday luncheons in their garden. We were usually a group of ten or twelve. Lunch was served under a spreading coihue tree. I'm sure the food was excellent, but to be truthful, I don't remember a thing about it. The big impact on my heart was the music—they always had a string quartet playing a classical piece—and, of course, laughter was its own kind of music. But above all, I see vases filled with flowers: just picked and arranged so informally. It is hard to be unhappy around flowers.

The lesson learned at that early age still guides me whenever I set a table or stage an event: Make sure there are flowers.

BEETS

LET IT BEET

The Spanish word for "beet" is *remolacha*.
What an enjoyable word to say! Your tongue
rolls around in your mouth like when you
say "ravioli" or "linguine." I truly came to
appreciate beets when I started cooking
with fire. Before that, when I was working in
Parisian kitchens, beets were almost a bad
word. "Why would you eat them?" my friends
in the kitchen would ask. "We use them as
feed for our pets and chickens." You'd only
find beets already boiled and sold in plastic
bags. I'd like to go back in time and tell
those long-ago kitchen comrades that beets,
like a shy person at a dinner party, have so
much personality if you are patient enough
to listen to them. They have a high level of
sugar, so if you boil them to bring out their
sweetness, then smash them on the plancha
(see page 119), you get a beautiful burnt
crust. They are also one of those foods that
have very little acidity or tanginess, so they
pair quite wonderfully with vinegar or citrus.
A few years ago, during a trip to Australia,
David Tanis (whose simple and wonderful
recipes appear regularly in the *New York
Times*) taught me to appreciate them raw,
grated and served in a salad. I do that a lot.

RESCOLDO BEETS WITH ORANGE, FENNEL, AND DILL SALSA

I think of this recipe as an intimate dinner party with three guests who are fond of one another, perhaps because they are different yet congenial. The beets bring char, smoke, and sweetness to the dish. The oranges, for their part, echo the sweetness of the beets and contribute acidity. Beets always like something tangy—whether from oranges, lemons, vinegar, or any other ingredients that can brighten the taste. And the fennel: well, he is a welcome guest because he is content to highlight the most pleasing aspects of his dinner partners. And, of course, fennel crunches so pleasantly. There are very few recipes that don't benefit from a little crunch.

Serves 4

4 beets

2 oranges

A handful of fresh dill leaves, finely chopped

1 small fennel bulb, finely diced

1½ teaspoons fennel seeds, toasted

¼ cup extra-virgin olive oil

Coarse salt

Prepare a fire and let the charcoal burn down to a bed of embers, coals, and ashes for rescoldo. As with all rescoldo cooking, you want a mix of warm ashes and some glowing embers, even a few coals to cover and surround the beets so that they char slowly as their insides cook through. Bury the beets in the embers, ashes, and coals and let them cook until tender all the way through when pierced with a skewer, about 1 hour. The timing will depend on the freshness and maturity of the beets.

If cooking indoors, preheat the oven to 400°F (200°C). Wrap each beet in foil and roast for about 1 hour, until they are tender all the way through when pierced with a skewer.

Meanwhile, make the salsa. Slice both ends off the oranges and, with a sharp knife, peel them through the pith right down to the flesh. Hold an orange over a bowl, cut the segments from between the membrane, letting the segments and juice fall into the bowl; discard the membrane. Repeat with the second orange. Tear the segments into small pieces and add the dill, diced fennel, and fennel seeds. Whisk in the olive oil and season to taste with salt.

When the beets are done, thoroughly brush off all the ashes and slip off and discard the skins. Wipe them with a wet paper towel if they are especially ashy. Cut the beets in half and arrange on a serving platter, with the salsa spooned over them.

SMASHED BEETS AND THEIR GREENS WITH GARLIC CHIPS AND VEGAN MAYONNAISE

If I were asked for an image that speaks my language of cooking, this dish expresses it well. The ingredients look destroyed, like fallen soldiers on the battlefield. But the forceful flavors in this chaotic tableau are very much alive when they hit your palate. Vegan mayonnaise—made with aquafaba—draws disparate tastes and textures together just like its nonvegan ancestor. Look for beets with lots of fresh, unwilted greens attached—fire loves them.

Serves 4

4 fresh young beets with their greens

Coarse salt

2 garlic cloves, peeled

A few rosemary sprigs

Extra-virgin olive oil

Red wine vinegar

Crispy Garlic Chips (page 296), for serving

Vegan Mayonnaise (page 294), for serving

Prepare a fire for very high heat and warm the plancha. (Or pull out a large cast-iron griddle if cooking indoors.)

Cut the greens off the beets and look for the nicest leaves to keep, discarding any bug-eaten or discolored ones. Rinse, pat dry, and reserve the greens on clean dish towels.

Place the beets in a deep saucepan with water to cover, salt the water, then add the garlic and rosemary. Bring to a boil and cook over medium heat for about 30 minutes, depending on the beets, until they are tender all the way through when pierced with a skewer. Drain and let sit until cool enough to handle.

Line a sheet pan with foil and have paper towels ready.

Place a beet between paper towels on a flat work surface. With the palm of your hand, slowly and gently smash the beet between the paper towels so the beet flattens but doesn't crumble apart. If it does, don't worry—just push it back together. With a wide spatula, transfer the smashed beet to the prepared sheet pan and brush with olive oil. Repeat with the remaining beets.

Brush the hot plancha with olive oil (if cooking indoors, heat the griddle over high heat, then brush with oil). When the oil shimmers, carefully add the beets without crowding them. Cook the beets until they are crisp and charred, about 2 minutes per side. Transfer them back to the sheet pan as they are done. Keep the plancha or griddle hot.

Oil the plancha or griddle again, and lay the beet greens on it; cook for about 1 minute. When you see patches of char on the bottom, sprinkle the greens with a little more oil and turn to briefly char them on the other side.

To serve, arrange the beets and the greens on a platter. Season to taste with vinegar, top with garlic chips, and serve with a bowl of vegan mayonnaise on the side.

BRAISED BEET AND PLUM SALAD

The combination of the warm crisped beets, raw sliced plums, and the unexpected punch of the chiles is what makes this salad so memorable. I see the plums as angels and the beets as little devils; prayers on the one hand, lust on the other. The gentle creaminess of the ricotta keeps this contrast under control.

Serves 4

4 beets

About 4 cups (1 L) vegetable broth, water, or a combination

2 garlic cloves, peeled

6 dill sprigs

2 tablespoons balsamic vinegar

Extra-virgin olive oil

Coarse salt

4 ripe red plums

1 cup (227 g) fresh ricotta cheese

1 or 2 small hot chiles, halved, ribs and seeds removed, and thinly sliced

Crunchy Breadcrumbs (page 297)

Heat the horno, or a home oven, to 375°F (190°C).

Place the beets in a small lidded pot or a baking dish deeper than the height of the beets. Pour in the broth to come about two-thirds up the sides of the beets. Add the garlic, half the dill, the vinegar, and olive oil and salt to taste. Put the lid on the pot or cover the dish tightly with foil and cook for about 1 hour, depending on the size of the beets, until they are tender all the way through when pierced with a skewer.

When the beets are cool enough to handle, cut them in half and brush generously with olive oil. Meanwhile, with a sharp knife, slice the plums as thinly as you can, cutting around the pit. Tear the remaining dill into pieces, discarding any tough stems, and set aside.

Prepare a fire for high heat and warm the plancha. If cooking indoors, heat a large cast-iron griddle over high heat.

Brush the hot plancha or griddle with olive oil. When the oil shimmers, add the beets cut side down. Cook until crisped on the bottom, about 2 minutes. Transfer to a wide platter.

Arrange the plums around the beets on the platter. Add dollops of ricotta, the sliced chiles, the breadcrumbs, and the remaining dill.

BEET, LENTIL, AND AVOCADO SALAD WITH CRUNCHY RICE

This recipe started with the idea of crispy rice as taught to me by an Iranian friend in Paris. We had spent a pleasant time drinking Negronis when, at one point, he said he was going to show me how to make a classic Persian rice. On the following Saturday, I accompanied him to an Iranian market where he had me savor the aromas of the wide array of rices. I chose some basmati with a sweet perfume. He cooked it up in a pot sealed with a cloth towel under the lid, with the result being a delicious crispy cake. This Patagonian recipe is a far cry from my friend's crispy rice, but somehow this combination of unctuous avocado, earthy lentils, sweet roasted beets, and crispy rice was born of the memory that began with an afternoon of cocktails in Paris. I often find that cooking takes one down such unexpected but rewarding pathways.

Serves 4 to 6

4 large beets

About ½ cup (118 ml) extra-virgin olive oil, plus more if needed

Coarse salt and freshly ground black pepper

1½ cups (300 g) lentils

1 large avocado

A handful of fresh cilantro leaves

Aioli (page 294)

FOR THE CRUNCHY RICE

1 tablespoon extra-virgin olive oil

1 onion, finely chopped

3 garlic cloves, smashed and peeled

2 cups (360 g) basmati rice

2 teaspoons fresh oregano leaves

2 teaspoons fresh thyme leaves

4 cups (475 ml) hot water

Coarse salt and freshly ground black pepper

Heat the horno, or a home oven, to 375°F (190°C).

Wrap the beets in foil, place them on a sheet pan, and roast for about 1 hour, depending on the size of the beets, until they are tender all the way through when pierced with a skewer. When the beets are cool enough to handle, slip off the skins and cut the beets in half. Place them in a bowl with any juices from the foil, a drizzle of olive oil, and salt and pepper to taste.

While the beets are roasting, heat the olive oil in a medium saucepan over medium-low heat. Add the onion and garlic and cook, stirring occasionally, until the onion is translucent, about 8 minutes. Add the rice, oregano, and thyme; stir to combine with the onion. Add the water—it should cover the rice by about half an inch (1.25 cm). Season with salt and pepper, bring to a boil, and cook for 2 minutes. Reduce the heat to a simmer and cook, covered, for about 15 minutes, until the rice is tender and has absorbed all the water. Set aside.

Meanwhile, put the lentils in a saucepan and cover with water by about 3 inches (8 cm). Bring to a boil, skim off any foam, and cook at a gentle simmer for about 20 minutes, or until the lentils are tender but not mushy and the liquid has reduced. Drain over a bowl, reserving the cooking liquid. Transfer the lentils to a separate bowl and dress them with olive oil, salt, and pepper to taste.

Prepare a fire for medium-high heat and warm the plancha. If cooking indoors, heat a large cast-iron griddle over medium-high heat.

Pour ¼ cup of the olive oil into a bowl. With a small sharp knife, peel the whole avocado and add it to the bowl, turning it to coat all sides. When the plancha or griddle is hot, brush it liberally with oil. When the oil shimmers, set the avocado on it to brown on one side, about 3 minutes. Turn it to brown on the other sides and set aside. Wipe off the surface of the plancha or griddle with an oiled paper towel.

Cut the beets in half and brush the cut sides with olive oil. Set them cut side down on the hot plancha or griddle until they are lightly charred and nicely crisped, about 3 minutes.

Wipe off the hot plancha or griddle again and brush it liberally with olive oil. When the oil shimmers, scoop cup-size portions of the rice onto the hot surface, using a spatula to flatten them into disks about ½ inch (1.25 cm) thick. Cook for a few minutes, until they are browned and crisp on the bottom, then carefully lift them with a wide spatula in each hand and turn them crust side up onto a large serving platter. Don't worry if they break apart; you can push them back together.

Add the lentils to the serving platter, moisten them with their reserved liquid, and top with cilantro leaves. Add the beets and the whole avocado. Spread the aioli over the crunchy rice, drizzle everything else with olive oil, and bring the platter to the table with a sharp knife to cut portions of the avocado.

BEETS AND ENDIVES

The charred bitterness of endives, in the months of autumn and early winter, is positively bracing—a fitting contrast to the beets, which overflow with sweetness like the bubbles of a hurriedly poured glass of champagne. Grated radishes lend a sharp tone.

Serves 4

4 beets

Coarse salt

2 tablespoons red wine vinegar

4 large garlic cloves, peeled

½ cup (118 ml) extra-virgin olive oil, plus more for drizzling

4 endives

Freshly ground black pepper

2 small spicy radishes

Prepare a fire for high heat and warm the plancha. (Or pull out a large cast-iron griddle if cooking indoors.)

Trim the beets, keeping about an inch (2.5 cm) of greens attached. Scrub well. Place in a deep saucepan with water to cover, salt the water, and add the vinegar and garlic. Bring to a boil, then cook over medium heat for about 30 minutes, depending on the size of the beets, until they are tender all the way through when pierced with a skewer. Drain in a colander. When cool enough to handle, cut the beets lengthwise in half. Transfer to a sheet pan and brush them generously with some of the olive oil on both sides.

Meanwhile, cut the endives lengthwise in half (or in quarters if they are large) and brush the cut sides with some of the olive oil. Season to taste with salt and pepper.

Brush the hot plancha with olive oil (if cooking indoors, heat the griddle over high heat, then brush with oil). When the oil shimmers, brown the endives on their cut sides until slightly charred, 1 to 2 minutes. Arrange on a serving platter.

Brush the plancha or griddle with more oil and cook the beets, cut side down, until nicely browned and crisp, about 2 minutes. Transfer to the platter and arrange among the endives. Drizzle with olive oil, then grate the radishes over the top.

CABBAGES (AND COUSINS)

SECRETLY SWEET, QUIETLY ELEGANT

Cabbages, Brussels sprouts, broccoli, and cauliflower, the botanists tell us, are all related. I didn't know that as a child, but like many children, I lumped them together anyway. What these vegetables had in common for me was the way they were cooked: often boiled until they were almost destroyed. Because cabbages are hardy and withstand the cold, they are among the few fresh vegetables available in fall and early winter. Maybe Brussels sprouts and broccoli weren't consumed with the same gusto as a delicate piece of leafy lettuce plucked from the garden and dressed with a sprightly vinaigrette, but at least these vegetables were a gratefully welcomed change from meat, potatoes, and dried beans. It wasn't until many years later, when I had stopped trying to make fancy French food for Buenos Aires sophisticates and was well into my love affair with fire, that I learned how elegant, smoky, and even sweet cabbage, Brussels sprouts, broccoli, and cauliflower can be when cooked slowly over fire. And how well they go with almost any sauce or garnish that you can imagine. I make them seared over a superhot plancha, long-smoked over the coals of a low fire, or roasted in my wood oven.

But before we light our fires, turn to page 130 for an exceedingly simple recipe that I eat nearly every day.

MY FAVORITE CABBAGE SLAW

People who know my work think first about live-fire meat cooking, but the recipe that I eat most often is this extremely simple salad served with a bowl of white rice. It has nothing to do with fire! My dear friend Jorge Donovan was sort of a father figure to me. He was probably the most famous Argentine fly fisherman ever. Although I have fly-fished a bit, I am not a fanatic about it. In 1982, my first restaurant and his fly shop shared a space in the Palermo Viejo neighborhood of Buenos Aires. We weren't open for lunch in those days, but during lunch hours, I would always be working, getting ready for dinner service. As time went by, Jorge and I became great friends, and we ate lunch together Monday through Friday. Jorge had a passionate Irish personality; when he laughed, which was often, his piercing blue-green eyes lit up. All throughout his life, he was always in great shape . . . very trim, perhaps because he loved to eat vegetables (and got a good workout wading our rushing Patagonian rivers). I think he preferred vegetables to a big steak. Almost until the end of his days, we ate lunch together, and he never tired of this salad. Here's to you, Jorge!

Serves 6

1 tablespoon red wine vinegar

1 tablespoon soy sauce

1 tablespoon fresh lemon juice

¼ cup extra-virgin olive oil

Coarse salt and freshly ground black pepper

1 red cabbage (about 2 pounds/1 kg), quartered

Hot basmati rice, for serving

Whisk together the vinegar, soy sauce, and lemon juice in a small bowl. Drizzle in the olive oil in a slow, steady stream, whisking constantly. Season to taste with salt and pepper.

Grate the cabbage on the largest holes of a box grater into a bowl. Add the vinaigrette and toss thoroughly to combine. Taste and adjust the seasoning, and serve with the rice.

WHOLE ROASTED CABBAGE WITH GRAPEFRUIT, WALNUTS, AND CAMPARI SALSA

The first time a diner sets eyes on the charred form of a whole roasted cabbage, their look is somewhat puzzled. That's part of the fun of this recipe. The unassuming hulk of cabbage has a certain austere beauty, promising little. As you cut into it and release a waft of steam and smoke, the puzzled look of your guests will turn into an expectant countenance, as if to say "I wasn't quite sure about this, but now I'm intrigued." What follows with the first bite is, quite often, rapture. All of this from a humble cabbage!

If you are contemplating a daylong cooking event (see The Dome, page 149), hang a cabbage over very low heat for many hours. If you don't have that amount of fire time, you can get quite nice results in an horno, or even a Weber kettle grill with a few coals banked along either side of the bottom of the kettle and the cabbage in the middle (where it is not receiving direct heat). If you don't have outdoor fire, you can get a nice result in a hot oven. Regardless of the heat source, my recommendation for the fullest flavor and the most dramatic presentation is to give the cabbage a good long cook time. I've cooked it for up to ten hours. Although I've never heard anyone compare a cabbage to a fine Burgundy, what holds true for both is that *flavor develops over time.*

Serves 6

1 green or red cabbage (about 2 pounds/1 kg)
¼ cup extra-virgin olive oil

FOR THE SALSA
1 pink grapefruit
½ cup (60 g) broken walnuts
¼ cup extra-virgin olive oil
2 tablespoons Campari liqueur
1 teaspoon chopped fresh rosemary

Heat the horno, or a home oven, to 350°F (180°C).

Trim off any damaged outer leaves from the cabbage and trim the core end so it sits flat. With a sharp knife, cut a deep X into the core and put the cabbage in a very large pot with plenty of water to cover. Bring to a boil over high heat, and blanch for about 5 minutes. Drain and pat the cabbage dry.

Pour the olive oil into a large deep cast-iron skillet or Dutch oven and roll the cabbage around in it until thoroughly coated. Cover the skillet or Dutch oven tightly with foil or a lid, place in the oven, and roast for about 30 minutes. At this point, check the cabbage for doneness by seeing how deeply you can pierce it with a long metal skewer or kitchen fork. This will give you an idea of how much more cooking time it needs. If the pot seems dry, add a little

water. Baste the cabbage with more oil and return it to the oven, uncovered, to roast for 40 to 60 minutes (depending on the size of the cabbage), or until it can be easily pierced all the way through.

Meanwhile, make the salsa. Using long-handled tongs and a pot holder, hold the grapefruit over a hot fire, rotating it occasionally, until the peel is spotted with char in patches, about 5 minutes. When the grapefruit is cool enough to handle, cut it into eighths and scrape the pulp and juice into a small bowl, discarding the seeds and membrane. Choose the two least-charred pieces of grapefruit peel and discard the rest. Set the peel down flat; with a small sharp knife, pare off all the bitter white pith, leaving only the zest. Finely chop the zest and set it aside.

Toast the walnuts in a small pan for about 5 minutes, until crisped and fragrant. Combine the olive oil, Campari, rosemary, grapefruit pulp and juice, and half the grapefruit zest in a bowl and whisk to combine. Taste and add more grapefruit zest only if you think it needs it.

To serve, set the cabbage on a carving board like you would a roast. Cut it in half through the core, lay the halves down flat, and carve them into wedges, keeping some core attached to each slice to hold them together. Spoon some salsa over the plated slices and serve the rest on the side.

TO COOK WITH THE DOME METHOD: Cook the whole cabbage hanging from the dome for 7 to 10 hours.

CABBAGE STEAKS, FOUR WAYS

When I first started following the path of a chef, nouvelle cuisine was all the rage in the world's top restaurants. The idea was to let the ingredients shine through rather than smothering them in sauces. Restaurateurs tried to outdo each other with clever names for their new and simple creations. You sort of jumbled up the names of different parts of a traditional menu and ended up with Mango Ravioli or Swordfish Parfait; it was all a bit silly. Nevertheless, the following recipes are indeed steaks—a whole roasted cabbage cut into thick slices and charred on a grill just as you might finish a sirloin steak. And in the same way that you can garnish a beefsteak with chimichurri, or any number of sauces, herbs, and toppings, I have yet to reach the limit of new toppings I can create for cabbage steaks. Try these, then follow your own whims; combine something sweet with something salty. Maybe add a touch of sourness, a bit of bitter, a dash of spicy heat. These fundamental tastes are your arsenal— deploy them as the spirit moves you.

Serves 4 to 6

1 whole roasted red or green cabbage
(see page 131)

6 tablespoons extra-virgin olive oil, plus more if needed

Coarse salt and freshly ground black pepper

Chimichurri (page 298), preferably made a day or so ahead of time

Prepare a fire for medium-high heat and warm the plancha. (Or pull out a large cast-iron griddle if cooking indoors.)

Oil a sheet pan.

Set the roasted cabbage on a cutting board core side down. Cut it in half straight through the core. Set one half down on its cut side. Starting at one end, slice it through the core into wedges about an inch (2.5 cm) thick. The core is what holds the steaks together, so try to keep as much as possible attached as you go. But if the wedges come apart at any point, don't worry— you can always push them back together. Lay the wedges out on the prepared pan, brush the tops with olive oil, and season to taste with salt and pepper.

Brush the hot plancha liberally with olive oil (if cooking indoors, heat the griddle over medium-high heat, then brush liberally with oil). When the oil shimmers, add the steaks, spacing them about an inch (2.5 cm) apart. Cook the cabbage steaks until browned and crusted on the bottom, 2 to 3 minutes. Using a sharp wide spatula, turn them to cook on the other side for about 2 minutes. To serve, arrange the steaks on individual plates or a serving platter. Drizzle some chimichurri over the steaks and serve the rest on the side.

VARIATIONS

CABBAGE STEAKS WITH MUSTARD-FENNEL CRUST

PICTURED ABOVE LEFT

Mustard gives you a touch of the piquance that cabbages always like, and fennel draws out their inherent sweetness.

½ cup (64 g) Dijon mustard

2 tablespoons fennel seeds, crushed

Coarse salt and freshly ground black pepper

6 tablespoons extra-virgin olive oil, plus more if needed

Paint the cabbage steaks with half the mustard, sprinkle with the fennel seeds, season to taste with salt and pepper, and drizzle with olive oil. Brush the remaining mustard onto a serving platter in broad strokes and set aside.

Liberally oil the hot plancha or griddle. When the oil shimmers, add the steaks mustard side down. Cook until they are browned on the bottom, about 2 minutes. With a sharp wide spatula, flip them over and cook on the other side for about 2 minutes. Lift the steaks onto the prepared serving platter and serve immediately.

continued

CABBAGE STEAKS WITH ORANGE CONFIT, GARLIC, AND MUSHROOMS

PICTURED ON PAGE 135, TOP RIGHT

Mushrooms pump up the savoriness of the cabbage, garlic adds nuttiness, and the orange peel lends some sweet/bitter floral notes.

½ recipe Orange Confit (page 296), with its oil

1 large portobello mushroom, very thinly sliced

2 large garlic cloves, very thinly sliced

2 tablespoons extra-virgin olive oil, plus more if needed

Coarse salt and freshly ground black pepper

Tear the orange confit into small pieces, reserving the oil. Arrange the sliced mushrooms in a layer on a serving platter.

Combine the garlic and 1 tablespoon of the olive oil in a small bowl and mix with your fingers to coat the garlic. Brush the remaining 1 tablespoon oil on the hot plancha or griddle and lightly brown the garlic on both sides, turning the slices over with a sharp metal spatula and lifting them onto a plate as they are done. Be careful not to burn them; they take less than a minute total.

Season the cabbage steaks to taste with salt and pepper, drizzle with more oil, and brown both sides on the hot plancha or griddle, about 2 minutes on each side. When the steaks are done, arrange them on top of the mushrooms and drizzle them with oil from the orange confit. Scatter the pieces of confit and the browned garlic over the top and serve.

CABBAGE STEAKS WITH ALMONDS, PARSLEY, HONEY, AND SOY

I love the crunch and nuttiness of the almonds, the fresh taste of the parsley, the sweetness of the honey that draws out the subtle sweetness of the cabbage, and the way soy sauce adds salinity and pungency.

1 lemon

½ cup (50 g) chopped toasted almonds

¼ cup extra-virgin olive oil

½ cup (25 g) chopped fresh parsley leaves

2 teaspoons honey, or to taste

2 teaspoons soy sauce, or to taste

Coarse salt and freshly ground black pepper

Zest the lemon into a small bowl and set the zest aside. Squeeze the juice from the lemon, strain out the seeds, and reserve the juice separately.

Place the almonds in another small bowl. Add the lemon juice, olive oil, parsley, honey, and soy sauce and mix together to make a coarse salsa.

Season the cabbage steaks to taste with salt and pepper and brown both sides on the hot plancha or griddle as described on page 134. Arrange the cabbage on a serving platter and drizzle with the salsa. Scatter the lemon zest over the top and serve.

SHAVED BRUSSELS SPROUT SALAD WITH CHERRY TOMATOES AND GARLIC

When my wife, Vanina, was the chef of 1884, my first restaurant in Mendoza (Argentina's premier wine region), she served this recipe. Instead of peeling off the leaves of a Brussels sprout, or serving it whole, she would shave the sprout into thin slices. That way, you get the crunch at the heart of the sprout and the smoother texture of the outside leaves, all in one bite. No fire necessary, just a simple dressing.

Serves 4 to 6

1 pound (454 g) Brussels sprouts

1 pint (300 g) cherry tomatoes, halved

1 or 2 garlic cloves, very thinly sliced or grated

¼ cup extra-virgin olive oil, plus more if needed

1 tablespoon soy sauce, or to taste

1 tablespoon red wine vinegar, or to taste

A pinch of crushed red pepper flakes, or to taste

Fleur de sel (optional)

Shave the Brussels sprouts on a mandoline (or slice them as thinly as possible with a knife) and place them in a salad bowl. Add the tomatoes and garlic and toss together.

Add the olive oil, soy sauce, vinegar, and red pepper flakes and toss again, using your hands to make sure the salad is well combined. If it seems dry, add more oil and vinegar. Taste carefully for salt and adjust the seasoning with a sprinkling of fleur de sel, if desired.

BRUSSELS SPROUT LEAVES A LA PLANCHA WITH LEMON AND CHILE

In Argentina our word for "Brussels sprout" is *repollito*: "little cabbage." Cooked and served whole, it tastes, unsurprisingly, like cabbage. But when the season of lacy lettuce and filigreed arugula is past, the supple leaves of Brussels sprouts serve as a light green. When done quickly on the plancha, some parts scorch, some brown a bit, and some stay vibrantly green and crispy. The leaves need no more than the simplest lemon vinaigrette, accented with spicy red pepper flakes.

Serves 4

1¼ pounds (600 g) Brussels sprouts

6 tablespoons extra-virgin olive oil, plus more for drizzling

Juice of 2 lemons

A pinch of crushed red pepper flakes

Fleur de sel

Prepare a fire for medium heat and warm the plancha. If cooking indoors, heat a large cast-iron griddle over medium heat.

With a sharp paring knife, slice off the stem ends of the Brussels sprouts, then pull off the leaves and drop them into a bowl. As the leaves get tighter, cut around the stem to release more leaves, slicing off more of the stem as you go. When you get to the core, discard it.

Brush the hot plancha or griddle with the olive oil. When the oil shimmers, add the Brussels sprout leaves (in batches, if necessary). Cook until the leaves are softened and lightly charred in patches, about 3 minutes. As the leaves are done, transfer them to a wide serving bowl and dress with the lemon juice, red pepper flakes, a good drizzle of olive oil, and fleur de sel to taste.

SCORCHED BRUSSELS SPROUT LEAVES WITH WALNUTS

There is a chef's rhyme that is a great guide to seasonal cooking: "If it grows together, it goes together." I completely agree; when the products of orchards, fields, and gardens mature at the same time, combining them is the most natural thing to do. In late autumn, Brussels sprouts and walnuts are at their peak, just waiting for us to marry them in this salad.

Serves 4

1 pound (454 g) Brussels sprouts

Extra-virgin olive oil

2 lemons: 1 juiced, 1 cut into wedges for serving

⅔ cup (150 g) walnut halves

Coarse salt and freshly ground black pepper

Prepare a fire for medium heat and warm the plancha. If cooking indoors, heat one or more cast-iron griddles over medium heat.

With a sharp paring knife, slice off the stem ends of the Brussels sprouts, then pull off the leaves and drop them into a bowl. As the leaves get tighter, cut around the stem to release more leaves, slicing off more of the stem as you go. When you get to the core, discard it.

Brush the hot plancha or griddle with olive oil. When the oil shimmers, add the Brussels sprout leaves (in batches, if necessary). Cook until the leaves are softened and lightly charred in patches, about 3 minutes. As the leaves are done, transfer them to a wide serving bowl and dress with the lemon juice.

Wipe the surface of the plancha or griddle with an oiled paper towel and scatter the nuts over it. Toast the nuts for about 1 minute, being careful not to burn them. Transfer to a cutting board and chop them very roughly, then add them to the bowl with the Brussels sprouts. Toss them together, season to taste with salt and pepper, and drizzle with olive oil. Serve with the lemon wedges on the side.

WHOLE ROASTED CAULIFLOWER WITH SESAME SEEDS, BURNT LEMON, AND ANTICA VERMOUTH

Some years ago, the Israeli chef Eyal Shani poached a whole cauliflower in milk, then roasted it in the oven until it was as brown as a dinner roll. Like many great ideas in cooking, once that recipe was released into the wild, chefs began to try their own variations of it. As with my Whole Roasted Cabbage (page 131), a dramatic presentation is important here. In the same way that a magnum of wine or a whole turkey makes a statement of generosity, bringing a whole cooked cauliflower to the table, then serving and dressing it where your guests can watch and anticipate, adds to the esprit of a shared meal. To my way of thinking, the rice and cauliflower in this dish are a calm presence set against the brightness and sharp flavors of the vermouth, lemon, spices, and herbs. Serve with Crunchy Rice (page 123).

Serves 2 as a main course, 4 as a side dish

Coarse salt

1 large cauliflower (about 2 pounds/1 kg)

3 tablespoons extra-virgin olive oil, plus more if needed

3 oregano sprigs, torn into pieces

Freshly ground black pepper

Crunchy Rice (page 123), for serving

FOR THE SALSA

1 lemon

1 tablespoon toasted white sesame seeds

1 tablespoon black sesame seeds

2 tablespoons Carpano Antica Formula vermouth or other sweet red vermouth

6 tablespoons extra-virgin olive oil, plus more if needed

1 tablespoon finely chopped fresh oregano leaves

2 tablespoons finely chopped fresh parsley leaves

Coarse salt

Heat the horno, or a home oven, to 400°F (200°C).

Bring a large pot of salted water to a boil over high heat. Set the cauliflower on its side on a work surface, cut off any damaged leaves, and trim the core end flat. Turn the core end upward and cut a deep X into it with a sharp knife. Lower the cauliflower into the boiling water, cover the pot, and bring the water back to a boil. Partially cover the pot and boil the cauliflower for 4 minutes. Drain thoroughly in a colander and pat completely dry.

Pour 1½ tablespoons of the olive oil into a 9- or 10-inch (23 or 25 cm) cast-iron skillet and roll the cauliflower around in it to coat well on all sides. Tuck small sprigs of oregano in between the florets here and there, season the cauliflower all over with salt and pepper, and slide the skillet into the oven. After 20 minutes, baste the cauliflower with additional olive oil, and rotate the skillet. Return the pan to the oven and roast until the cauliflower is golden brown and tender, about 30 minutes longer, or until it can easily be pierced all the way through with a metal skewer. Baste with additional olive oil and rotate the skillet as needed as it roasts. If necessary,

increase the oven temperature toward the end to help it brown.

While the cauliflower is roasting, make the salsa. Pierce the lemon through the middle with a long kitchen fork and roast it on all sides over a medium fire (or stovetop burner) until it is tender all the way through, about 8 minutes. Cut it into quarters and, with a sharp teaspoon, scoop the pulp and juice into a small bowl, discarding the seeds and membrane. Lay the peel down on a work surface and scrape off and discard all the bitter white pith, leaving only the zest. Chop the zest and set aside separately. Crush most of the sesame seeds, leaving about a teaspoon of each color whole.

Place the vermouth in a small bowl. Add 1 teaspoon of the lemon zest, the oregano and parsley, the crushed sesame seeds, and the lemon juice and pulp. Stir in the remaining olive oil and add salt to taste. If desired, add more lemon zest or olive oil.

To serve, place the whole cauliflower on a bed of crunchy rice. Spoon a little of the salsa on top and serve the rest in a small bowl alongside. Carve the cauliflower into wedges at the table.

BROCCOLI A LA PLANCHA WITH SUN-DRIED TOMATOES

When cooked on the plancha, broccoli retains a bright freshness that is a far cry from the way it was boiled into submission in the cafeteria of my school (perhaps your school as well). The florets soften while the stems retain a bit of snap and crispness. A bit of char here and there strikes a powerful note. Try my version of simple sun-dried tomatoes before you reach for store-bought.

Serves 4

1 large head of broccoli

Coarse salt

¼ cup extra-virgin olive oil, plus more for drizzling and the plancha

¼ cup finely chopped fresh parsley leaves

Juice of 1 lemon

Coarsely ground black pepper

12 Sun-Dried Tomatoes (page 295)

Fleur de sel

Prepare a fire for high heat and warm the plancha. (Or pull out a large cast-iron griddle if cooking indoors.)

Slice the broccoli, including the stems, lengthwise into large pieces. Pare or scrape off any tough skin on the stems. Bring a large pot of lightly salted water to a rolling boil and blanch the broccoli for 1 minute. It should turn bright green. Immediately drain it in a colander under cold running water to stop the cooking and pat it dry with a clean dish towel. Transfer to a sheet pan and drizzle with olive oil.

Whisk together the parsley, lemon juice, the ¼ cup olive oil, and pepper to taste in a small bowl. Set aside.

Brush the hot plancha with olive oil (if cooking indoors, heat the griddle over high heat, then brush with oil). When the oil shimmers, add the broccoli in a single uncrowded layer. Cook until the broccoli is charred and crisp on the first side but the stems still have some bite, several minutes. Flip and repeat on the other side.

To serve, arrange the sun-dried tomatoes on a wide platter and scatter the broccoli over the top. Drizzle the parsley mixture over it and sprinkle with fleur de sel.

The Dome

It's a skeleton of iron over a ring of fire. Some nights, tired and smoky from sixteen hours of cooking, I lie in bed and think, *After a fifty-year friendship with fire, it has come to this.* In such moments, I am tired but never weary. A silence creeps over me like a caress—gentle yet somehow fierce. I see my dome, silhouetted against the sky, where food hangs from its encircling bands like ornaments from a Christmas tree.

And just as Christmas is a special occasion, a full-on dome event is, for me, a celebration—of a marriage, a birth, a gathering together of friends. A dome is much more than making a meal. Instead, it is a process that begins early, usually at eight in the morning after my breakfast of coffee, homemade bread, and butter from my neighbor's cow (who always looks at me as if she is pleading for something, perhaps just a pet on her flanks). Then I build my fire. Hugging the circle of iron, the mounting flames rise through the hardwood logs to lick the twigs and branches as the smoke billows. No time for dreamy speculation, though. Time to hang the first fruits and vegetables: cabbages, pineapples, bunches of beets, carrots. Sometimes all of these, sometimes whatever is at hand.

At the two-hour mark, it's time to festoon the dome with broccoli, cauliflower, bunches of

grapes or bananas, fennel. If you have them all, consider yourself wealthy and use them.

By now, you should have some embers and ashes for rescoldo: if you have potatoes (white or sweet or both) or onions, bury them rescoldo-style and cook according to the rescoldo recipes in this book.

When four hours have passed, hang the leafy vegetables, such as chard and kale.

After one more hour, remove the fruits and vegetables, taking them in reverse order (the last shall be first!).

Contemplating this canopy of black iron hung with the harvest of the garden and the fruits of a nearby orchard, I will often sit on a chair, in the leafy shade of a tree, and, almost like a voyeur, I'll feast my eyes on the eternal process of heat and smoke seeping into the flesh of these trophies. Our ancestors, stretching back past the dawn of time, have bequeathed to us this fascination with flame. At such times— on the precipice of life and hope—I'm happy, anticipating tastes and smells, succulence and crispness. No time for worries. My cares disappear and my thoughts speak in the language of fire. It is poetry composed of flame and wind,

the slow sounds of sizzle and drip, the rattling of the crumbling embers of seasoned wood on glowing coals; the transformation of the vibrant colors of the harvest into the muted blacks, browns, and gold of food baptized by fire: sensuous, carnal, delicious.

In a time where technology takes us further and further from the living world, the age-old task of tending a cooking fire is rooted in our senses: our intuition, our hands, our mouths, our bellies. The scientists who delve deeply into such matters tell us that before we stood fully upright, before we invented spears and arrows, it was fire that enabled us to take the first steps that made us truly human. Deep thoughts. But staring at a fire has this effect.

Having cooked with fire in every imaginable way, I find that it is the dome that sums things up for me. The story began ten years ago with hanging a haunch of lamb from the bough of a tree over the embers of a campfire. I quickly discovered that almost any fruit or vegetable can be suspended over flames to be like-wise transmuted into a stunning, satisfying, smoke-seasoned, gently cooked dish. A whole cabbage, after hours on the dome, fairly longs to be steaked, grilled on the plancha, and fin-ished with a topping (see page 131). A pine-apple melts to peach-like softness, ready for a mantle of ice cream and berries (see page 272).

Dome cooking has taken me to Madrid's Plaza Mayor, a park in Brooklyn's Williamsburg, the cliffs of Big Sur, a hill in Hong Kong with a view toward Repulse Bay, and the snowy peaks of the Rockies. No matter how far away I take my dome, there is always a place in my heart where iron, smoke, wind, and the silence of sunset bear me back to my beloved Andes.

Homeward bound.

CARROTS

SHY, BUT BEAUTIFUL

Carrots are like a superb actor whom you see in many movies, but only in supporting roles: familiar but rarely as celebrated as the leading players. Carrots are one of the so-called aromatics that are the foundation of French, Italian, and Spanish cuisine. Whether you know the combination as mirepoix, battuto, or soffrito, so many classic recipes call for sautéing onions, celery, and carrots as a first step. But like poor Cinderella, whose true beauty is hidden in the tattered outfit of a scullery maid, carrots are rarely noticed in fancy recipes. For me, the beauty of carrots revealed itself as I first learned about the versatility of potatoes cooked with live fire. Like potatoes, carrots come in all sizes and colors. Likewise, they play well with almost any combination of herbs. They char beautifully when finished over high heat. Perhaps chief among this root vegetable's virtues is the way cooking unlocks the sweetness that resides in every carrot—barely noticed until fire transforms it. A roasted carrot finished on the plancha is like Cinderella when she finally makes her dazzling debut at the grand ball—a true beauty.

PICTURED OPPOSITE: BODEGA GARZON

YOUNG CARROTS A LA PLANCHA WITH CHARRED MINT AND GREEN GARLIC SALSA

Young carrots cook up relatively quickly on the plancha—sweet yet crisp. At the same time of year that one harvests these carrot infants, green garlic and garlic scapes make their appearance as well. When carrots are tossed with a charred herb salsa, the effect is bracingly fresh, crunchy. Mint, though not sweet, has a way of encouraging the sweetness of other ingredients to come out for a visit on your palate. If you can't find green garlic or it's not in season, use scallions.

Notes:
- *If your young carrots come with their tender greens attached, by all means grill them as well.*
- *Young carrots are long and slim. So-called baby carrots—which have become popular for dipping in hummus or salsa—are not babies at all. They are made from mature carrots that are cut into sections and turned on a lathe-like machine. I don't use them.*

Serves 4 to 6

2 to 3 pounds (1 to 1.5 kg) young carrots, assorted colors if you can find them

About ⅔ cup (160 ml) extra-virgin olive oil, plus more if needed

Coarse salt and freshly ground black pepper

A handful of mint sprigs, tied together with kitchen twine

A handful of tender green garlic shoots, garlic scapes, garlic chives, or scallions

Juice of 1 large lemon

1 bunch parsley, chopped

Good-quality red wine vinegar

A small pinch of crushed red pepper flakes

Prepare a fire for medium heat and warm the plancha. (Or pull out a large cast-iron griddle if cooking indoors.)

Trim the tops of the carrots, scrub them well, and slice them lengthwise in half. Brush them with 2 tablespoons of the olive oil and season to taste with salt and black pepper. Set aside on a sheet pan with the bundle of mint.

If the green garlic is on the thick side, slice it lengthwise. If using garlic scapes, cut crosswise into 6-inch (15 cm) lengths. If using garlic chives, pat them dry and tie them lightly together with kitchen twine. Whichever you are using, add them to the sheet pan and drizzle everything with olive oil.

Brush the hot plancha with olive oil (if cooking indoors, heat the griddle over medium heat, then brush with oil). When the oil shimmers, add the mint and the green garlic and cook until partially charred on the bottom, about 2 minutes. Baste the uncooked side of the herbs with olive oil and turn them over with tongs; cook for another minute or so to lightly brown the other side. The green garlic or garlic scapes should be somewhat softened. As they are done, transfer them to a large cutting board, then cut and discard the twine. Trim off and discard any tough stems and chop the garlic together with the mint. Scrape into a bowl and drizzle with the lemon juice. Mix in the parsley and drizzle generously with olive oil and splashes of vinegar to taste. Season this salsa carefully with salt, black pepper, and red pepper flakes.

Wipe off the plancha or griddle and brush with olive oil. Spread out the carrots on the hot surface and cook for several minutes on both sides, until tender. To serve, transfer them to a serving dish and spoon the salsa over them.

CHARRED CARROTS WITH BLACK QUINOA AND MINT

I have read that the Indigenous peoples of South America have been cultivating quinoa for at least five thousand years, but somehow the grain escaped the attention of most chefs and home cooks until the last twenty years or so, when it began to be touted as an ancient superfood. I really don't know much about what constitutes a superfood, and when I first tasted quinoa I found it bland. My wife, Vanina, however, began to cook with it at 1884, my original Mendoza restaurant, and later at her own place, Maria Antonieta. Through her I learned to appreciate black quinoa in particular, because it remains crunchy when cooked. The chorus of textures that results from the encounter of quinoa, carrots, and avocado hits all the right contrasting notes.

Serves 4

Coarse salt

1 cup (170 g) black quinoa, thoroughly rinsed and drained

2 tablespoons extra-virgin olive oil, plus more for drizzling

6 medium carrots

About 3 cups (700 ml) vegetable stock or water

A few thyme sprigs

4 garlic cloves, peeled

1 tablespoon red wine vinegar

Freshly ground black pepper

1 large avocado

Juice of 2 lemons

A small handful of fresh mint leaves

Prepare a fire for medium-high heat and warm the plancha. (Or pull out a large cast-iron griddle if cooking indoors.)

Meanwhile, bring a large pot of salted water to a boil over medium-high heat. Add the quinoa and boil until the white germ ring is visible and the quinoa is tender but not mushy, 10 to 15 minutes. Drain in a fine-mesh strainer, transfer to a bowl, and toss with a good drizzle of olive oil. Arrange on a wide platter and set aside.

Cut off all but an inch (2.5 cm) of greens from the carrots, peel or scrub them well, and cut them in half on the diagonal. Place them in a large skillet and add enough stock to almost cover them. Add the thyme, garlic, the 2 tablespoons olive oil, and the vinegar and season to taste with salt and pepper. Cook, partially covered, over medium heat until the carrots are tender but still firm, 5 to 8 minutes; drain any excess liquid.

Brush the hot plancha with olive oil (if cooking indoors, heat the griddle over medium-high heat, then brush with oil). When the oil shimmers, add the carrots. Cook until they are well browned on the bottom, about 3 minutes, then baste with a little olive oil and turn them to brown the other side.

Arrange the carrots on top of the quinoa. Halve and pit the avocado, then scoop out the flesh with a tablespoon, arranging it around the carrots. Dress with lemon juice and olive oil, and scatter the mint leaves over the top.

CARROTS CHIRINGUITO

I put this recipe in the category of "beach food": it's simple, quick, and casual. We serve these carrots at my restaurant Chiringuito, down by the seaside in José Ignacio, Uruguay. *Chiringuito* is a word that is used affectionately to describe an open-air beach shack that serves food ("restaurant" is almost too fancy a word for such eateries). This recipe is a good example of how you can use a larger plancha to cook different ingredients separately.

Labneh or yogurt is served with cooked carrots throughout the Middle East. My view of traditional combinations of ingredients is that they must be good if people have eaten them together for centuries.

Serves 4

1 bunch carrots (reserve the tenderest carrot tops separately)

Extra-virgin olive oil

1 tablespoon fresh thyme leaves

6 small hot or mild sweet peppers, such as shishito or mini peppers (see headnote, page 28)

¼ cup shelled pistachios, toasted

½ cup (118 ml) plain yogurt or labneh, chilled

Prepare a fire for medium heat and warm the plancha. If cooking indoors, heat a large cast-iron griddle over medium heat.

Meanwhile, thinly slice the carrots lengthwise.

Brush the hot plancha or griddle with olive oil. When the oil shimmers, add the carrots and a handful of carrot tops, spreading them out on the hot surface. Cook until they are charred in patches, 3 to 5 minutes, then turn and cook on the other side for a minute or so to soften them slightly. Sprinkle with the thyme.

Meanwhile, brush a separate part of the plancha (or another griddle) with oil. Add the peppers and lightly brown for several minutes. Using two wide spatulas, toss the carrots and peppers together, then transfer them to the serving platter. Scatter the pistachios over the top and serve with the cool yogurt.

BRAISED CARROTS WITH GARLIC AND ROSEMARY

As winter deepens its grip on the land, you often find carrots that are quite large. They take a good long while to cook, but the reward is deeply sweet. When the carrots are tender all the way through, reduce any of the braising liquid that remains. It is so delicious. As a finishing touch, garlic chips add a nutty nuance.

Serves 6

6 large carrots, about 3 pounds (1.5 kg), well scrubbed (or peeled if necessary)

1 head of garlic cloves, separated

A small bunch of rosemary

About 2½ cups (600 ml) warm vegetable stock, plus more stock or water if needed

¼ cup extra-virgin olive oil

1½ tablespoons red wine vinegar

Coarse salt and freshly ground black pepper

Crispy Garlic Chips (page 296)

Heat the horno, or a home oven, to 400°F (200°C).

Choose a heavy metal roasting pan that will hold the carrots comfortably in one layer with the stock. Arrange the carrots in the pan, and tuck the garlic and most of the rosemary sprigs in between and around the carrots. Pour in enough stock to come about halfway up the sides of the carrots; add the olive oil, half the vinegar, and salt and pepper to taste; then roll the carrots around in the liquid to moisten them.

Roast the carrots for 30 to 40 minutes, until they are very tender all the way through when pierced with a fork and golden brown on top, 1 hour or more, depending on the size of the carrots. Make sure to check them occasionally and add more liquid if needed.

When the carrots are done, place the roasting pan over medium-high heat and reduce any remaining braising liquid until it is rich and silky. Transfer to a serving dish with the remaining rosemary sprigs and a light sprinkling of the remaining vinegar, and top with the garlic chips. Serve immediately.

CARROTS WITH CREAM AND THYME

I am, by some standards, a French-trained chef making gaucho cuisine. This recipe—quite simple—showcases both sides. The carrots are cooked in a skillet on a parrilla with a reduction of thyme-infused cream, a time-honored French way of adding flavor and texture.

Serves 6

Coarse salt

6 large carrots, peeled and sliced into ½-inch-thick (1.25 cm) rounds

1 tablespoon extra-virgin olive oil, plus more if needed

1 cup (237 ml) heavy cream

2 tablespoons fresh thyme leaves

Prepare a fire for high heat and set a grate over it.

Meanwhile, bring a large pot of salted water to a boil over high heat. Add the carrots and boil for 3 minutes. Drain thoroughly.

Brush the surface of a large cast-iron skillet lightly with olive oil and set the skillet over the grate (or over medium heat on the stovetop, if cooking indoors). When the oil shimmers, add the carrots, working in batches if necessary. Cook until they are browned on the bottom, about 2 minutes, then turn and brown them on the other side. If you cooked them in batches, return all the carrots to the skillet and slowly add half the cream. Cook until the cream has reduced by half, 2 to 3 minutes. Add the remaining cream and the thyme and toss together with the carrots using two spatulas. Cook until the cream thickens and blends with the carrots, then serve.

Christmas in the Southern Hemisphere

For South Americans, Christmas comes a few days after Midsummer Eve, a far cry from wintry landscapes, stories of Santa Claus and his sleigh, and *A Christmas Carol*. Still, the iconic snow-covered Christmas has always had a powerful hold on the popular imagination. For years I would do a roast beef or a properly kitted-out goose for our holiday dinner. However, when my daughters Ambar and Allegra became vegan a few years back, roast meat was no longer on the Christmas menu. Instead, I make a mélange of root vegetables, long-cooked carrots, potatoes, squash, fennel, garlic—whatever is at hand that will take kindly to long, slow roasting. Like any true preparer of a Christmas feast—even if you're not roasting a big piece of meat—part of the journey to the plate requires the cook to open the oven from time to time, to fuss a bit with whatever you're cooking. "Is it done yet?" is an eternal question at holiday feasts. These vegetables are perfectly cast to play that role. Roast them for a long while so some parts become soft and others crisp. Turn them from time to time so they brown on the outside and get meltingly soft on the inside.

CHRISTMAS VEGETABLES

Note: The vegetables should be a collection of the ones you and your family love the most, whole or cut into large pieces so they all end up done at the same time.

Serves 8 to 12

4 medium carrots, scrubbed

3 fennel bulbs, trimmed lengthwise and cut into wedges

4 sweet potatoes, halved or quartered lengthwise

4 red onions, quartered

Squash (any type), unpeeled and cut into wedges

2 small Italian eggplants

8 heads of garlic, halved crosswise

1 bunch thyme

1 bunch rosemary

Coarse salt and freshly ground black pepper

About ½ cup (118 ml) extra-virgin olive oil, plus more as needed

Heat the horno, or a home oven, to 325°F (170°C).

Combine the vegetables, garlic, and herbs in a large roasting pan. Season to taste with salt and pepper. Add the olive oil and toss together. Place in the oven and roast for about 2 hours, turning occasionally, and adding more oil if needed, until the vegetables and garlic are browned, tender, and very fragrant.

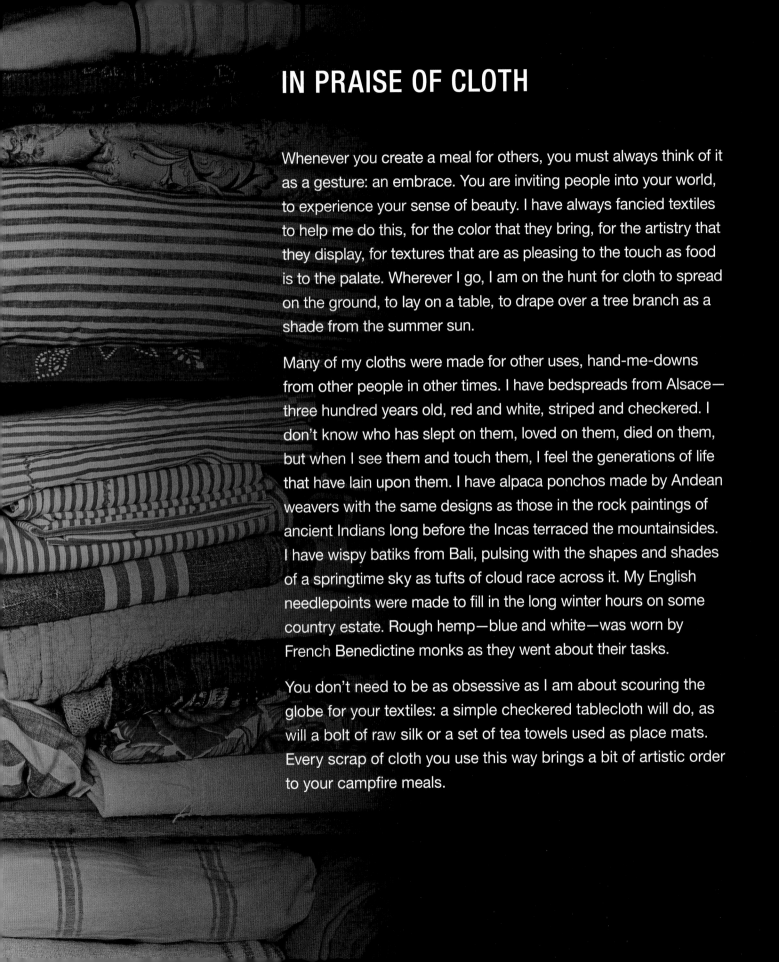

IN PRAISE OF CLOTH

Whenever you create a meal for others, you must always think of it as a gesture: an embrace. You are inviting people into your world, to experience your sense of beauty. I have always fancied textiles to help me do this, for the color that they bring, for the artistry that they display, for textures that are as pleasing to the touch as food is to the palate. Wherever I go, I am on the hunt for cloth to spread on the ground, to lay on a table, to drape over a tree branch as a shade from the summer sun.

Many of my cloths were made for other uses, hand-me-downs from other people in other times. I have bedspreads from Alsace—three hundred years old, red and white, striped and checkered. I don't know who has slept on them, loved on them, died on them, but when I see them and touch them, I feel the generations of life that have lain upon them. I have alpaca ponchos made by Andean weavers with the same designs as those in the rock paintings of ancient Indians long before the Incas terraced the mountainsides. I have wispy batiks from Bali, pulsing with the shapes and shades of a springtime sky as tufts of cloud race across it. My English needlepoints were made to fill in the long winter hours on some country estate. Rough hemp—blue and white—was worn by French Benedictine monks as they went about their tasks.

You don't need to be as obsessive as I am about scouring the globe for your textiles: a simple checkered tablecloth will do, as will a bolt of raw silk or a set of tea towels used as place mats. Every scrap of cloth you use this way brings a bit of artistic order to your campfire meals.

CORN

THE GOLDEN GODDESS OF THE AMERICAS

If you were to drive from Times Square in New York City to my home in La Boca, Buenos Aires, you would pass through mountains, seashores, grassy plains, and thick jungle. What do such different landscapes have in common?

For thousands of years, Native Americans grew corn along every mile of the journey.

Corn was worshipped as a golden-haired goddess. Corn represented fertility. It represented art. In short, corn was life, and life was unthinkable without corn. It was ground into grits, scraped and milked straight off the cob, dried and stewed, stirred as tirelessly as risotto (and with the same creamy results). I have cooked corn the way the Aztecs did and—closer to home—the way the Incas would, leaving it out in the mountain air to freeze and thaw for days on end until they stewed it into something creamy and smoky. In Italy, I learned the art of polenta, and in the province of Salta, in the north of Argentina, I saw how the Indigenous people crushed corn between two enormous stones and drained off the pulp and elixir of the fresh kernels. They wrapped it in the tenderest leaves of the husk and cooked it on the plancha, in a wood oven, or on a parrilla over a low fire.

Wherever fire was tamed, the first peoples of the Americas cooked corn.

HUMITAS, THREE WAYS

Humitas are the Andean cousin of the familiar tamale of Mexico and Central America. Where tamales are stuffed with masa (dried cornmeal), humitas are filled with grated fresh corn. There are still many Inca people in the north of Argentina, and I first learned the Inca way to make humitas in the mid-1980s while filming one of my early television shows. I always liked to go on location, especially with our Indigenous peoples. It was a very cold day in the mountains of Santa Fe. We had made filming arrangements with a local woman who was a renowned "humitress." Bundled up in layers of clothing to ward off the frigid air and wearing a beautiful apron, she welcomed us. She grated corn on a stone that had been used by her people for centuries whenever they wanted to pulverize or grate an ingredient. Meanwhile, she boiled the corn husks so they were supple enough to wrap around the mixture of grated corn, chiles, onions, and a bit of cheese. In the cold mountain air, her humitas were a welcome bit of warmth. If you're wondering where the corn husks are in this recipe, you won't find them here. I decided to go straight for the delicious innards.

Serves 4 to 6

8 ears fresh corn, shucked

2 tablespoons unsalted butter

1 tablespoon extra-virgin olive oil, plus more for drizzling

1 medium onion, chopped

½ cup (118 ml) whole milk

A handful of whole fresh basil leaves

1 teaspoon crushed red pepper flakes

Coarse salt and freshly ground black pepper

A pinch of sugar (optional)

Toasted country bread, for serving

Prepare a fire for medium-low heat and set a grate over it. Pull out a medium deep cast-iron pot, such as a caldero or Dutch oven.

Using the large holes of a box grater, grate the corn kernels off the cobs into a large bowl.

Run the dull edge of a knife down each cob after grating to scrape all the sweet, milky liquid from the cobs into the bowl.

Set the caldero or Dutch oven on the grate (or over medium-low heat if cooking indoors). Warm the butter and olive oil, then add the onion. Cook gently, stirring, until the onion is translucent, about 8 minutes. Don't let it brown.

Stir in the corn and its liquid and continue to cook for a minute or two, until the liquid begins to thicken. Stir in half the milk, and when it has been absorbed, gradually stir in the remaining milk. Simmer over low heat, stirring, for about 5 minutes, depending on the corn, until the kernels are cooked and the mixture is thick.

Thinly slice or chop the basil and stir it into the corn. Add red pepper flakes to taste, and season with salt, black pepper, and a pinch of sugar or a light drizzle of olive oil, if desired. Serve with toasted bread on the side.

VARIATIONS

HUMITAS WITH PINE NUTS AND CAPERS

If you consider the list of ingredients in a chef's recipe, you can often tell a bit about that person's history. In my case, this recipe combines the humitas of the Andes with a classic condiment of the Mediterranean that you'll find in the old Italian neighborhoods of Buenos Aires.

Serves 4

3 scallions, trimmed

1 tablespoon capers, drained

1 tablespoon extra-virgin olive oil, plus more for the plancha

¼ cup pine nuts, toasted

Slices of toast, for serving

Make the humitas as on opposite page.

Brown the scallions on a hot oiled plancha or skillet until partly charred and slightly softened. Remove from the heat and roughly chop. Set aside. Place the capers in a small bowl and stir in a tablespoon or so of olive oil. Add the scallions and pine nuts. Spoon the topping over the warm humitas and serve with toast.

continued

HUMITAS A LA PARRILLA IN CHARRED CHARD

Classic humitas are wrapped in corn husks, but the husks are too tough and stringy to eat. So I bundle mine in chard, which is more edible. I particularly like the bit of smokiness that you get from the charred chard. Adding melted cheese inside is a favorite way of preparing humitas in the province of Salta in the north of Argentina. Going back to my early twenties, I have learned so much from Salteño cuisine.

Serves 4

8 large perfect leaves of Swiss chard, with stems

4 ounces (113 g) soft, fresh goat cheese, crumbled

½ cup (118 ml) extra-virgin olive oil, plus more if needed

Make the humitas as on page 182, omitting the olive oil.

Prepare a fire for high heat and set a grate over it for the caldero. (Or pull out a large pot and a ridged cast-iron grill pan if cooking indoors.)

Fill the caldero with water for blanching, set it on the grate, and bring to a rolling boil (or fill the large pot with water and bring to a boil on the stovetop if cooking indoors). Line a sheet pan with dish towels.

Meanwhile, tie the chard leaves together by the stems with string. Holding the bundle by the stems with tongs, dunk it briefly into the boiling water until the leaves soften but remain bright green, half a minute or less. Shake off the water and transfer to the prepared sheet pan. Cut the string and lay the leaves out flat and pat them completely dry.

Open the leaves out flat on a cutting board. With a sharp knife, trim out the toughest part of the stems, cutting a deep V around them into the leaf base. Spoon about 3 tablespoons of the humitas onto the widest part of each leaf. Make a well in each with the back of a spoon and fill with 1 tablespoon of the cheese, then cover the cheese with the humitas. Fold the sides up over the filling and roll up the leaves to form packets. Brush generously with olive oil on all sides.

Brush the hot grill grate with olive oil (if cooking indoors, heat the grill pan over high heat, then brush with oil). Arrange the packets on the grill, seam side up, and cook until the bottoms are charred and release easily, 1 to 2 minutes. Using a wide spatula, turn and grill on the other side for another minute or so, until the chard is charred, the packets are heated through completely, and the cheese is melted. Transfer to individual plates and serve immediately.

CREAMY POLENTA
WITH GRILLED MUSHROOMS

In 1985, my first book was published. I was so proud of it, especially the picture of a wonderful polenta recipe on the cover. So, for a culinary festival in Buenos Aires, I planned to demonstrate this recipe. The audience of about a hundred people filled the huge tent where the cooking demo was to take place. The event was completely sold out. Imagine my surprise and disappointment when I announced that I was going to demonstrate polenta and half the audience got up and left before I even started. It seemed that the food snobs of Buenos Aires didn't want to learn anything about polenta, which they considered poor people's food. Although we've made some progress against such food snobbery, whenever I write something about polenta, I often get a lot of comments like: "Mallmann must be broke if he's writing polenta recipes instead of steak." Such people forget that in humble kitchens, where every penny counts, home cooks have learned to create truly captivating flavors and textures from the simplest ingredients. To me, such heritage dishes are the true basis of great cooking.

Serves 4

5 cups (1.18 L) whole milk (or half milk, half water), plus more if needed

½ cup (118 ml) extra-virgin olive oil, plus more for the parrilla

1½ cups (240 g) medium or coarse polenta

2 tablespoons unsalted butter, cut into pieces

1½ cups (150 g) grated Parmesan or cheddar cheese

1¼ pounds (600 g) cleaned and trimmed mixed mushrooms, such as shiitake, portobello, oyster

3 garlic cloves, finely chopped

A large handful of fresh parsley leaves, chopped

Coarse salt and freshly ground black pepper

Crushed red pepper flakes (optional)

Prepare a fire for medium-high heat and set a grate over it. Pull out a large deep cast-iron pot, such as a caldero or Dutch oven. Set the pot on the grate (or on the stovetop over medium-low heat if cooking indoors).

Put the milk and 2 tablespoons of the olive oil into the pot, and bring to a boil. Gradually stir in the polenta, continuing to stir as it thickens. Adjust the coals (or the stovetop) to lower the heat, and cook the polenta at a gentle bubble, stirring every few minutes and adding more milk or water if needed, until the polenta is smooth, thick, and creamy but still quite moist, about 20 minutes. Remove it from the heat and, with a wooden spoon, beat in the butter, then the cheese. Cover and keep warm, stirring occasionally, and add hot milk or water by the spoonful if necessary while you grill the mushrooms.

If using oyster mushrooms, break up any extra-large clumps before grilling. Place the garlic in a bowl with the parsley. Stir in the remaining olive oil and season to taste with salt and pepper and red pepper flakes, if using. Brush the hot grill grate with oil and add the mushrooms in a single layer, in batches, if necessary (if cooking indoors, heat the grill pan

over high heat, then brush with oil). Cook over high heat until nicely browned, about 2 minutes. Baste with the oil from the garlic and parsley mixture, then turn and cook on the other side until the mushrooms are tender and juicy when pierced with a fork, about 2 minutes longer. As they are done, transfer them back to their bowl with the garlic and parsley. If using whole portobellos, cut them in half or quarter them with scissors over the bowl to catch the juices. Toss the mushrooms with the garlic and parsley mixture, adding more oil if desired. Spoon the mixture over bowls of warm polenta and serve immediately.

GRILLED POLENTA SLICES WITH CHARRED SPINACH AND CHILES

Whenever I visit my refuge on a little island in the remotest outback of Patagonia, I often make a batch of polenta that I store in loaf pans and eat for days. In winter, when the snow is piled in huge drifts outside my cabin door, I'll bury the loaf pans in the snow until I'm ready to slice the polenta, grill it, and feed a campful of guests and relatives. As a main course or a side dish, polenta slices accept an enormous variety of toppings and sauces. Chances are, if you can dream it up, it's going to be filling and delicious. Here the lightly scorched spinach pairs well with the bright and sweet mini peppers.

Serves 4 to 6

2 cups (475 ml) vegetable stock or whole milk

2 cups (475 ml) water

1 tablespoon extra-virgin olive oil, plus more for the plancha

1½ cups (240 g) medium or coarse polenta

Coarse salt and freshly ground black pepper

8 tablespoons (113 g) unsalted butter, cut into pieces

1 cup (100 g) freshly grated Parmesan cheese

2 or 3 bunches cleaned spinach, tough stems removed

Juice of 2 lemons

4 small sweet fresh chiles, cored, seeded, and thinly sliced crosswise

Fleur de sel

First make the polenta. Line a 9 by 13-inch (23 by 33 cm) sheet pan with plastic wrap. Combine the stock, water, and olive oil in a pot and set over medium-high heat. Stir in the polenta, bring to a boil, and cook, stirring frequently, until the polenta is thick enough to hold its shape, about 15 minutes. Season to taste with salt and pepper. Remove from the heat and beat in the butter a few pieces at a time with a wooden spoon, then add the Parmesan. Spread the polenta onto the prepared sheet pan, cover the surface with plastic wrap, and pat it down flat. Refrigerate for about 1 hour until firm, or up to a day ahead of time. When ready to cook, unmold the polenta and cut into 12 pieces.

Prepare a fire for high heat and warm the plancha. If cooking indoors, heat a large cast-iron griddle over high heat.

Brush the hot plancha or griddle with olive oil. When the oil shimmers, add the polenta slices about an inch (2.5 cm) apart. Cook until nicely browned, about 2 minutes on each side. Transfer them to a large serving platter as they are done.

Wipe off the plancha or griddle and brush it with oil again. When it just starts to smoke, use tongs to spread the spinach out over the whole surface. The spinach should start to wilt and brown on the bottom—cook it on one side just long enough for the stems to soften. Using tongs, transfer the half-cooked spinach to a serving platter and drizzle with the lemon juice. Scatter the sliced chiles over it, sprinkle with fleur de sel, and serve immediately.

GRILLED POLENTA
WITH RADICCHIO AND ARUGULA

This is a knife-and-fork sandwich. Polenta with a generous amount of Parmesan perked up by the peppery sharpness of radicchio and arugula. To my way of thinking, it's an ideal mix of tastes and textures. It never resolves into a single taste. Instead, each of these ingredients maintains its identity until you swallow it. It's a little combat that's fought to an appealing draw.

Serves 4 as a main course, 8 as an appetizer

2 cups (475 ml) whole milk or vegetable stock

2 cups (475 ml) water

5 tablespoons extra-virgin olive oil, plus more for drizzling

1½ cups (240 g) medium polenta

8 tablespoons (113 g) unsalted butter, cut into 1-inch (2.5 cm) pieces

1 cup (100 g) freshly grated Parmesan cheese

A large handful of arugula

A small head of radicchio, leaves separated and sliced into wide strips

Red wine vinegar

Coarse salt and freshly ground black pepper

First make the polenta. Line an 8-inch (20 cm) square cake pan with plastic wrap. Combine the milk, water, and 1 tablespoon of the olive oil in a pot over medium-high heat and bring to a boil. Gradually stir in the polenta and cook, stirring, until the polenta becomes thick and creamy, about 20 minutes. Beat in the butter and Parmesan with a wooden spoon. Spread the polenta mixture into the prepared pan, cover with another sheet of plastic wrap, and flatten the polenta down into an even layer with a spatula or the palm of your hand. It should be about an inch (2.5 cm) thick. Refrigerate for at least 1 hour until firm, or for up to a day.

Prepare a fire for medium-high heat and warm the plancha. If cooking indoors, heat one or more large cast-iron griddles over medium-high heat.

Cut the chilled polenta into quarters, then cut the quarters in half to form eight rectangles total. Brush the hot plancha or griddle generously with the olive oil and arrange the pieces of polenta on it, spaced well apart. Cook until browned on the bottom, about 3 minutes, then turn and brown the other side for about 3 minutes, adding more oil to the plancha if needed. The pieces should be browned on the outside and warm inside.

Meanwhile, toss the arugula and radicchio together in a bowl and dress with the remaining olive oil, the vinegar, and salt and pepper to taste.

To serve, set the polenta slices on individual serving plates. With a sharp-edged spatula, slice through the grilled polenta and open it like a bun. Fill it with a layer of the arugula and radicchio salad and replace the top. Serve immediately.

GRILLED CORN SALAD WITH AVOCADO AND CHERRY TOMATOES

From 2000 to 2006, when Argentina was going through one of its frequent financial crises, I made my home in Quogue on the East End of Long Island. I had a sweet little auberge on a quiet street and a restaurant on the beach in Westhampton. It was bathed in magical Long Island light that diffuses through gentle sea mist. The growing season is longer on the East End than it is inland because of the warming effect of the Gulf Stream. I have a vivid taste memory of the sweet corn there: grilled until charred in spots, browned in others, and swollen with sweetness all over. Intensely flavorful cherry tomatoes, creamy avocado, and the accents of fresh herbs combine in this salad to remind me of those seaside summers.

Serves 6

6 ears very fresh corn, shucked

¼ cup extra-virgin olive oil, plus more if needed

1 pint (290 g) cherry tomatoes, halved

Coarse salt

A handful of fresh cilantro leaves

A handful of fresh parsley leaves

3 avocados

Juice of 3 lemons

Freshly ground black pepper

Chile Oil (page 299, optional)

Prepare a fire for high heat and set a grate over it. If cooking indoors, heat a ridged cast-iron grill pan over high heat.

Brush the corn with some of the olive oil and oil the grill grate or grill pan. Grill the corn, turning occasionally, for 5 to 10 minutes, depending on how much char you like on your corn. Transfer to a cutting board and slice the kernels off in long strips.

While the corn is grilling, place the cherry tomatoes in a bowl and sprinkle them with salt to taste. Add the cilantro and parsley leaves, drizzle with some of the olive oil, and toss lightly together.

Meanwhile, slice the avocados into rounds: Hold an avocado on its side on a cutting board and, with a sharp serrated knife, start cutting off ¾-inch-thick (2 cm) slices right through the skin. When you reach the pit, just cut around it—the slices will slip right off onto the cutting board. Peel the slices, and brush them with lemon juice so they don't discolor.

To serve, arrange the corn, tomatoes, and avocados on a wide serving platter. Dress with lemon juice, olive oil, salt, and pepper, and drizzle with chile oil, if desired.

GRILLED CORN SALAD WITH MUSHROOMS, ARUGULA, AND SWEET PEPPERS

When corn is in season, I can eat it nearly every day. The interesting twist here is the mushrooms. Grilled then doused with this light vinaigrette, they are smooth and slide across your palate like ravioli. Mushrooms have some magical savory property that elevates the flavor of every other ingredient in this salad. The corn and the peppers are that much sweeter, the arugula that much sharper.

Serves 6

1 pound (454 g) shiitake mushrooms, cleaned, stems removed

½ cup (118 ml) extra-virgin olive oil, plus more if needed

2 garlic cloves, finely chopped

6 ears very fresh corn, shucked

2 tablespoons chopped shallot

Coarse salt and freshly ground black pepper

5 ounces (142 g) arugula leaves

A few mini sweet peppers, sliced

2 tablespoons red wine vinegar

Prepare a fire for medium-high heat and set a grate over it. If cooking indoors, heat a ridged cast-iron grill pan over medium-high heat.

Toss the mushrooms in a bowl with ¼ cup of the olive oil and the garlic. Set aside.

Brush the corn with some of the olive oil and oil the grill grate or grill pan. Grill the corn, turning occasionally, for 5 to 10 minutes, depending on how much char you like on your corn. Transfer to a cutting board and slice the kernels off in long strips, then chop them up a bit and add them to a bowl. Stir in the shallot and season to taste with salt and black pepper.

Brush the grill grate or grill pan with more olive oil. Arrange the mushrooms, cap side down, on the grate or pan in a single layer. Cook for 2 minutes, then baste with garlic oil from the bowl and turn them over, cap side down, and baste with more garlic oil. Grill the caps until nicely marked on the bottom and tender and juicy when pierced with a fork, about 2 minutes. As they are done, add them (and the rendered liquid in the cap) to the bowl with the corn. Using scissors, cut the larger caps into big pieces over the bowl to capture their liquid. Toss together with a bit more salt and black pepper to taste and let stand for a few minutes.

To serve, place the arugula and sliced peppers in a large salad bowl and dress with the remaining olive oil, the vinegar, and salt and black pepper to taste. Toss the corn and mushrooms together with any liquid in the bowl and add it to the arugula and peppers.

FENNEL

A GENIAL COMPANION

I was quite unaware of fennel until I worked in the town of Imola, Italy, at San Domenico, a Michelin three-star restaurant owned by Gianluigi Morini. Despite its august haute cuisine recipes, San Domenico is often credited with elevating the rustic traditions of the trattoria to the ranks of fine dining. I was in my early twenties at the time, and my goal was to become a fancy chef back home in Argentina, but I think the rustic sentiment must have lodged in my memory, because that is what I would eventually do when I took the traditions of gaucho and Indigenous cuisine and combined them in elegant settings. My philosophy: As long as a recipe is satisfying, it doesn't matter how humble its origins—it still deserves the most beautiful ambience and accouterments.

At San Domenico, there was a very popular dish of roast pig and fennel pollen served with fennel confit. I paid little attention to this unfamiliar vegetable at the time, even though I must have prepared a thousand servings as I worked on the line. It wasn't until I turned to wood fire that fennel revealed its simple, intense beauty. Roasted, burnt, raw, braised, or confited, it has a pleasing mild taste. And although it is not particularly sweet, it has an ability to reveal the subtle sweetness in other ingredients. As many a teacher has said about a cooperative young student, fennel "plays well with others."

FENNEL SALAD WITH MINT

As the months of winter grind on . . . and on . . . and on, I long for the crunch of a fresh salad. I am thankful at that time to find that fennel is often still in the market and quite amenable to playing the lead role in this fresh-tasting salad. Fennel has a slight anise or licorice component, as does mint, but somehow they are admirably restrained and don't overpower your palate.

Serves 6

3 fennel bulbs
Extra-virgin olive oil
1 lemon
A handful of fresh mint leaves
Fleur de sel

Trim the fennel bulbs, discard the stalks and any tough core, and cut them in half from root to stem. Slice lengthwise as thinly as possible, preferably on a mandoline.

Place the fennel in a bowl and drizzle with olive oil. Grate the lemon zest over the fennel, then cut the lemon in half and squeeze the juice over the top. Add the mint leaves, season to taste with fleur de sel, and toss gently before serving.

BURNT FENNEL AND CHERRY TOMATOES A LA PLANCHA WITH AVOCADO AND SUNFLOWER SEEDS

Earthy, nutty, rich, piquant, sweet, salty, crunchy—this recipe is a sampler of many tastes and textures. Every ingredient retains its identity so that the overall effect is like that of a group of friends with strong personalities gathered together in spirited conversation.

Serves 6

FOR THE LIMONETA

¾ cup (175 ml) extra-virgin olive oil

¼ cup fresh lemon juice

Coarse salt and freshly ground black pepper

3 fennel bulbs

Extra-virgin olive oil

3 small ripe avocados

10 ounces (300 g) cherry tomatoes, halved

2 tablespoons sugar

Coarse salt

¼ cup toasted sunflower seeds

Fleur de sel

Prepare a fire for medium heat and warm the plancha. If cooking indoors, heat a large cast-iron griddle over medium heat.

To make the limoneta, measure the olive oil into a small bowl and stir in the lemon juice with a fork. Season to taste with salt and pepper. Set aside.

Slice the fennel bulbs lengthwise about ½ inch (1.25 cm) thick and lay them out on a sheet pan. Brush them generously on both sides with olive oil. Brush the hot plancha or griddle with oil and arrange the fennel slices on it, giving them plenty of space. Cook until they are well browned on the bottom, about 5 minutes. Turn and cook on the other side until just tender in the middle, 3 to 5 minutes. As they are done, transfer them to a wide serving platter in a single layer.

Meanwhile, slice the avocados into rounds (see page 192) and dress them lightly with 2 tablespoons of the limoneta. When the fennel is done, arrange the avocado slices on top of the fennel on the platter.

Oil the plancha or griddle again and add the cherry tomatoes, cut side down. Sprinkle them with the sugar and a little salt and cook for several minutes without disturbing them. With a sharp-edged spatula, turn the tomatoes and brown them for about 30 seconds on the other side (you don't want them to burst). Transfer them directly to the serving platter with the fennel and avocado. Scatter the sunflower seeds over the top, and dress with the remaining limoneta and fleur de sel to taste.

BURNT FENNEL A LA PLANCHA WITH COGNAC, CORIANDER, AND CARDAMOM SALSA

Charring the fennel on a plancha gives it an attractive look and a bit of toastiness, while the interior of each fennel slice cooks to the cusp of softness with some remaining crunchiness. Coriander and cardamom seeds—which go so well with fennel—add a bit of pungency to the salsa, which, like all good dressings, complements the star of the show. As for the cognac, it's always a nice gesture.

Serves 4 to 6

3 large fennel bulbs, trimmed

2 tablespoons extra-virgin olive oil, plus more for the plancha

Coarse salt and freshly ground black pepper

1½ teaspoons fennel seeds

FOR THE SALSA

½ teaspoon green cardamom seeds (from about 8 pods)

1½ teaspoons coriander seeds

2 tablespoons cognac

1 tablespoon honey

1 teaspoon fresh thyme leaves

⅓ cup (75 ml) extra-virgin olive oil

¼ teaspoon red wine vinegar

Coarse salt

Prepare a fire for medium-high heat and warm the plancha. (Or pull out a large cast-iron griddle if cooking indoors.)

Cut the fennel bulbs lengthwise into ½-inch-thick (1.25 cm) slices, slicing through the base to hold them together. Set them on a sheet pan, add the olive oil, and turn to coat them well on both sides. Sprinkle with salt, pepper, and the fennel seeds, and set aside.

To make the salsa, drop the cardamom seeds into a small dry skillet. Add the coriander seeds and toast over medium heat for about 3 minutes, stirring until they are fragrant. Transfer the seeds to a mortar and crush them, then return them to the skillet. Reduce the heat, add the cognac, avert your head, and touch a lit match to it to flambé. When the flame subsides, stir in the honey and thyme. Remove from the heat, stir in the olive oil and vinegar, and season to taste with salt.

Brush the hot plancha with olive oil (if cooking indoors, heat the griddle over medium-high heat, then brush with oil). When the oil shimmers, arrange the fennel slices on the surface. Cook on the first side until nicely charred, about 3 minutes. Turn and cook on the other side until the slices are tender when pierced with a fork.

To serve, arrange the fennel on a serving platter and spoon the salsa over it.

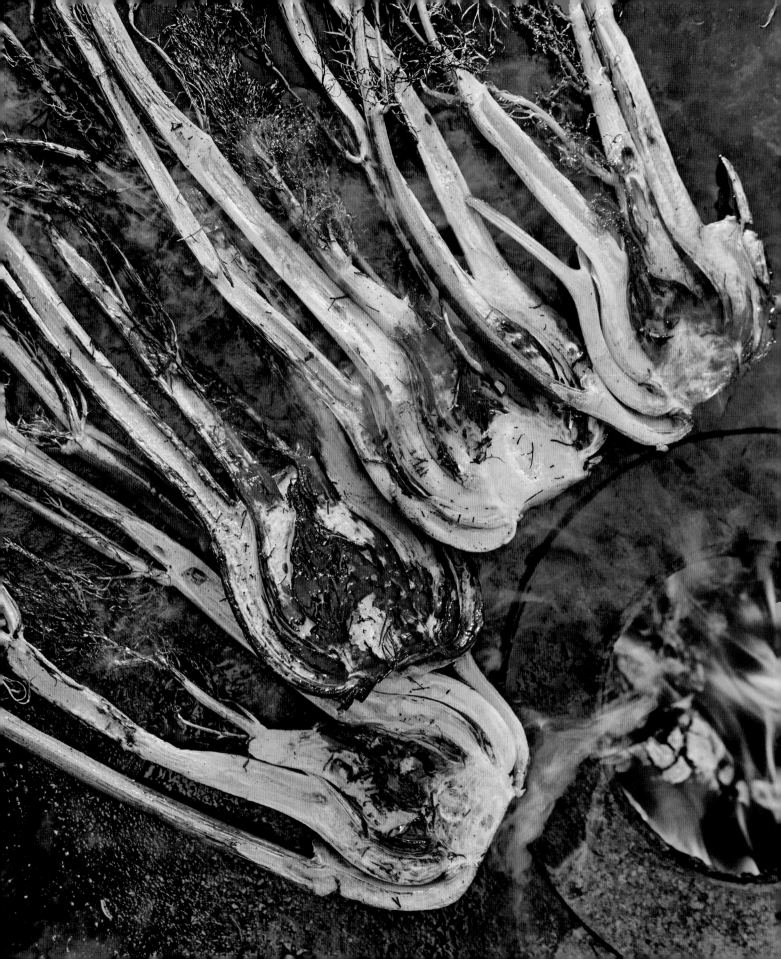

FENNEL CONFIT WITH JAMMY EGGS

When you confit fennel, it gets soft and succulent: almost melted. The coriander seeds, cardamom, and rosemary add flashes of aromatic flavor. Jammy eggs are sublime—filled with soft yolk that can't decide if it wants to be a liquid or a solid, so it stakes out a position clearly in the middle. Although fennel is not typically a breakfast ingredient, I find that this recipe makes a lovely late breakfast, a light lunch, or an equally light dinner.

Serves 6

1 cup (237 ml) extra-virgin olive oil

3 fennel bulbs

1 head of garlic, cut in half crosswise

1 tablespoon coriander seeds

2 bay leaves

6 cardamom pods

3 large rosemary sprigs

1 teaspoon coarse salt

8 whole black peppercorns

1½ cups (354 ml) water

3 eggs

Lemon wedges, for serving

Heat the horno, or a home oven, to 375°F (190°C).

Pour ½ cup (118 ml) of the olive oil into a small Dutch oven. Arrange the fennel bulbs in it and add the garlic, coriander, bay leaves, cardamom, rosemary, salt, and peppercorns. Add the remaining ½ cup (118 ml) olive oil and the water. Cover the pot and bake for about 1 hour, until the fennel is very tender when pierced all the way through with a skewer.

Meanwhile, fill a saucepan with enough water to cover the eggs and bring to a boil over medium heat. Lower the eggs into the water and boil for 6 minutes. Using a wide spider or skimmer, transfer the eggs directly to a large bowl of ice and water to stop the cooking. Crack the shells and peel the eggs.

When the fennel is done, remove it from the oil and slice it into rounds. Cut the eggs into rough pieces. Arrange the fennel slices on a platter, scatter the eggs on top, and serve with lemon wedges alongside.

FENNEL RAGOUT

As I learned through years of making ratatouille, if you have a bunch of vegetables in season, it's hard to misstep by combining them in a stew or ragout. Serve with a creamy polenta and you have a hearty vegetarian meal.

Serves 4

2 large fennel bulbs, trimmed, feathery fronds reserved

¼ cup extra-virgin olive oil, plus more if needed

1 large red onion, halved and thinly sliced

2 medium zucchini or yellow squash, diced

5 garlic cloves, roughly chopped

5 ripe, meaty large tomatoes, chopped into large pieces, juices reserved

A handful of fresh dill leaves, roughly chopped

Coarse salt and freshly ground black pepper

Good-quality red wine vinegar

Crushed red pepper flakes

Creamy Polenta (page 186)

Prepare a fire for low heat and set a grate over it.

Slice the fennel bulbs in half lengthwise, then into thin lengthwise slices. Set a large cast-iron skillet on the grate (or on the stovetop over low heat if cooking indoors); add the olive oil and onion; and cook very gently, stirring, until the onion is translucent. Increase the heat to medium. Add the zucchini and cook for a minute or two to lightly brown, then add the sliced fennel and garlic and cook, stirring, for a few minutes longer, taking care not to burn the garlic or onion.

Pour in the tomatoes and their juices and cook until the vegetables are tender and have released all their juices into the ragout. Add the dill and most of the fennel fronds and cook for another minute or two to blend the flavors and reduce the liquid; remove from the heat. Season to taste with salt and black pepper and add a hit or two of vinegar and red pepper flakes to taste. Top with the remaining fennel fronds and serve over polenta.

PAN CHATO WITH FENNEL

Pan chato is our Argentine version of flatbread, beloved of gauchos who will take their long knives and cut off a piece of meat while it is roasting and wrap it in the flatbread. No plates or forks necessary. Pan chato is quite wonderful with many different toppings of herbs and vegetables. For this one, I roll it up with a filling of fennel, olives, and tomatoes, just like a roulade or a jelly roll. The bottom crisps up, and the wonderful vegetable mix stays in place (otherwise, all those bits on an unrolled chato could end up in your lap!).

Serves 6

FOR THE DOUGH

1 teaspoon active dry yeast

About ¾ cup (175 ml) lukewarm water

About 2 cups (240 g) flour, plus more
for dusting

1½ teaspoons coarse salt

1½ teaspoons sugar

¼ cup extra-virgin olive oil

FOR THE TAPENADE

1 cup (155 g) pitted kalamata olives

2½ tablespoons (30 g) drained capers

¼ cup extra-virgin olive oil, plus more if needed

2 fennel bulbs, trimmed, tough core removed

1 onion

3 drained Tomatoes Confit (page 65), or
1½ cups (270 g) drained canned tomatoes

To make the dough, dissolve the yeast in ¼ cup of the warm water. Combine the flour, salt, and sugar in the bowl of an electric stand mixer with the paddle attachment and mix on low speed. Add the yeast mixture, olive oil, and another ¼ cup warm water and mix until combined. Gradually add up to 6 more tablespoons of water to form a dough that comes together without being too sticky or too dry. Switch to the dough hook and knead on medium speed for about 8 minutes, until the dough is smooth and elastic. Place it in a large floured bowl; cover with a damp cloth; and let rise in a warm place for about 1 hour, or until almost doubled.

Prepare a fire for medium-high heat and warm the plancha. (Or pull out a large cast-iron skillet if cooking indoors.) Heat the horno, or a home oven, to 375°F (190°C).

Chop the olives and capers and mix them together in a bowl. Add 2 tablespoons of the olive oil and mix to combine. The mixture should be spreadable but not too oily. Set aside.

Cut the fennel bulbs in half lengthwise, then very thinly slice the halves lengthwise on a mandoline. Place in a bowl and toss with about 2 tablespoons olive oil. Cut the onion in half lengthwise and slice it about ¼ inch thick, transfer it to a separate bowl, add a drizzle of olive oil, and toss to coat.

Line a sheet pan with paper towels.

Brush the hot plancha or griddle with oil (if cooking indoors, heat the skillet over medium-high heat, then brush with oil) and add the sliced fennel in an even layer. Cook until golden brown on the bottom, about a minute, then turn with a wide metal spatula to brown the other side.

Transfer to the paper towel–lined pan. Brush the plancha or skillet with more olive oil and cook the sliced onion on both sides in the same manner. Reserve separately while you shape the dough.

Flour a work surface, and line a large sheet pan with parchment. Set the dough on the floured surface and flatten it with the palms of your hands. Then, with your fingers, carefully push and stretch it out into a long oblong about ⅛ inch (3 mm) thick.

Spoon the tapenade onto the dough and spread it out, leaving a 1-inch (2.5 cm) margin on all sides. Distribute the tomatoes on top of the tapenade, then the fennel, and finally the onion. Lift one long side of the dough and start rolling it up over the filling as though you were making a jelly roll. Flour the work surface again if necessary and position the dough seam side down. Using a sharp knife, trim off the excess dough from one end, slice the roll into ¾-inch-thick (2 cm) rounds, and transfer to the prepared sheet pan, spaced about 1 inch (2.5 cm) apart.

Bake for about 20 minutes, or until nicely browned. Serve hot.

BEANS

OF HORSES AND HARVESTS

I once had a little farm on a hill in the seaside town of José Ignacio—quite near my beachfront restaurant, Los Negros. Etelvino Nievas, the man who looked after the farm, also made my clay ovens. Etelvino had an unusual way of cleaning the beans that he harvested each year. He would gather them and place them on a hilltop on a piece of burlap, where they would dry in the warmth of the sun and the sea breeze. After a week or two, he would get on his horse and walk it back and forth over the beans and, in so doing, separate the edible kernels from the tough husks. The next time the wind blew, it would pick up the husks and scatter them, leaving the delicious kernels. If the weather was fine, he'd let the beans dry in the sun for another week or two.

For those of you who don't have a seaside farm, a string of horses, and a bean field, you will—as I do—buy your beans already dried, and here is where you can be easily disappointed if the beans have not been picked in the most recent season. If they are old, no amount of soaking and simmering will render them creamy, smooth, and succulent. There are some brands in which I always have confidence, such as Rancho Gordo. You may also have good luck if there are dried beans on offer at a local farmers' market. Don't for a minute think of buying those sad-looking bags that are on the bottom shelf at the supermarket.

In the depths of winter, few things warm my spirit more than the sight and smell of a pot of beans simmering for hours over a low fire. Time and patience are two things that are often overlooked in our fast-paced society. And in summer, fresh beans are a sign of the fullness of the season.

CHAUCHAS A LA PLANCHA WITH CUCUMBER VINAIGRETTE

Although we often think of beans as dried and hard pantry items requiring long simmering, these summer beans are quite the opposite and taste as fresh as anything in the garden. Our Argentine nickname "chaucha" encompasses fresh green, wax, and romano beans, which are often seen in adjacent heaps at farmers' markets. A quick blanching—which can be done earlier in the day—precooks them and sets the color while retaining garden-fresh taste. A visit to the plancha imparts some char and caramelization. As with many fruits and vegetables harvested at their peak, fresh beans require few additional ingredients to produce a flavorful and nuanced dish. Cucumber and a vinaigrette add a refreshing finish.

Serves 4

1 pound (454 g) mixed young, tender beans such as green, wax, and romano, trimmed

¼ cup extra-virgin olive oil, plus more for the plancha

1½ tablespoons red wine vinegar

1 small cucumber, peeled, seeded, and finely diced

Coarse salt and freshly ground black pepper

Prepare a fire for medium-high heat and warm the plancha. (Or pull out a large cast-iron griddle if cooking indoors.)

Meanwhile, bring a large pot of water to a rolling boil and add the beans. Return to a boil and cook for about 30 seconds (the beans should turn a bright green). Drain in a colander and run under cold water to cool.

Whisk together the oil and vinegar in a bowl. Stir in the cucumber, then season to taste with salt and pepper.

Brush the hot plancha with oil (if cooking indoors, heat the griddle over medium-high heat, then brush with oil). Spread the beans over the hot surface and cook without disturbing them until they are lightly charred in patches, 2 to 3 minutes. Using two wide spatulas (one in each hand), toss the beans, then brown the other side. They should be tender but still have a good bite. Add half the cucumber vinaigrette to the beans and toss together like a salad. Transfer to a wide, shallow serving dish and toss with the remaining vinaigrette. Season to taste and serve.

GRIDDLED BLACK AND WHITE BEAN SALAD

Some years after I started making smashed potatoes by boiling potatoes and then slowly crusting them up on the plancha (see page 27), I realized you can cook beans by simmering them and then finishing them on the plancha for a nice crust. Any time you can add crunch to a dish, the recipe becomes more interesting. I like the look of two different-colored beans for this salad. I find that black ones are more intensely flavored and whites a little lighter in taste. Fennel and scallion cut through with a bit of sweetness and piquance.

When crusting the simmered beans, spread them out so that all of them come into contact with the hot plancha—and don't move them. You only need to crisp them on that one side. The black and white beans should be cooked separately and tossed together at the end, otherwise the black beans will discolor the white ones.

Note: Save the flavorful broth when draining the beans to drink or to add to soups.

Serves 4 to 6

1 cup (140 g) dried black beans

1 cup (140 g) dried white beans, such as cannellini or great northern

1 red onion, quartered

12 whole black peppercorns

8 thyme sprigs

2 large bay leaves

1 head of garlic, halved crosswise

½ cup (118 ml) extra-virgin olive oil, plus more if needed

1 large fennel bulb, halved lengthwise, fronds reserved

Coarse salt and freshly ground black pepper

1 bunch scallions, sliced on the diagonal

2 tablespoons red wine vinegar, plus more if desired

A large handful of fresh parsley leaves

Soak the beans in two separate bowls filled with water for at least 6 hours or overnight.

Prepare a fire for medium-high heat and warm the plancha. (Or pull out two large cast-iron griddles if cooking indoors.)

Meanwhile, drain and rinse the beans separately, and place in separate pots. Cover with plenty of water, then add 2 onion quarters, 6 peppercorns, 4 thyme sprigs, 1 bay leaf, and half the garlic to each pot. Set over medium-high heat, bring to a boil, and cook for about 25 minutes, depending on the beans, until tender but not mushy. Drain the beans separately and spread them out on separate sheet pans to cool. Drizzle lightly with some of the olive oil and toss gently to coat. Set aside.

While the beans are cooking, slice the fennel halves lengthwise about ½ inch (1.25 cm) thick, cutting through the root end to keep the slices intact. Place in a bowl and toss them with 2 tablespoons of the olive oil. Season to taste with salt and pepper. Line a sheet pan with paper towels. Brush the hot plancha with olive oil (if cooking indoors, heat one griddle over medium-high heat, then brush with oil), then grill the fennel slices until nicely browned, about 5 minutes. Turn and brown the other side for about 3 minutes, and transfer to the prepared pan.

Add some more oil to the hot plancha or griddle and add the scallions. Cook until lightly browned on the bottom, about 1 minute, and transfer to a serving bowl.

Oil the plancha again and spread the beans in two separate areas. If cooking indoors, oil the griddle you used for the scallions as well as a second griddle. Cook the beans on one side only until crispy on the bottom, about 2 minutes.

When the beans are done, season them while still on the plancha with the vinegar and some salt, tossing the black and white beans together with two wide metal spatulas. Then transfer them to the serving bowl with the scallions and add the parsley leaves. If cooking indoors, season them with vinegar and salt on their separate griddles and transfer to the bowl to toss. Drizzle with olive oil and add more vinegar, salt, and pepper to taste. Top with the grilled fennel and the reserved fronds and serve warm.

GRIDDLED CHICKPEA SALAD

The centuries of Moorish rule in Spain left the Hispanic world with an appreciation of chickpeas. Whether dried then ground to serve as a flour, or soaked and simmered whole, they are an efficient vehicle for flavors. As in the bean salad on page 220, I crisp the cooked chickpeas on the plancha. You get more concentrated flavor if you drizzle them with some of their broth when you first put them on the plancha. The broth will reduce and glaze the chickpeas as they crisp up. Eat the salad warm right after it's taken off the griddle.

Serves 6 to 8

2 cups (180 g) dried chickpeas

Coarse salt

2 bay leaves

6 large garlic cloves, peeled

3 lemons

A large handful of fresh basil leaves

A large handful of fresh parsley leaves

½ cup (118 ml) extra-virgin olive oil, plus more for the plancha

1½ teaspoons whole black peppercorns, coarsely crushed

2 tablespoons red wine vinegar

1 red onion, finely chopped

Soak the chickpeas in a large bowl filled with water for at least 12 hours or overnight.

Drain and rinse the chickpeas. Place them in a deep pot, cover with plenty of water, season with salt to taste, and add the bay leaves and garlic. Bring to a boil over high heat, then let the chickpeas bubble gently over low heat until tender, anywhere from 30 minutes to an hour or more, depending on the freshness of the chickpeas. Drain thoroughly, reserving about ½ cup (118 ml) of the broth, and spread the chickpeas out on a sheet pan to dry.

Prepare a fire for medium-high heat and warm the plancha. (Or pull out a large cast-iron griddle if cooking indoors.)

Meanwhile, make the salsa. Place the lemons in a saucepan, cover with water, and bring to a boil over high heat. Cook for 2 minutes. Drain and repeat two more times. The third time, cook them for 30 minutes. Drain and cool. (This process removes bitterness from the lemons.) Cut them into quarters and, with a teaspoon, scoop the pulp and juice into a small bowl, discarding the seeds and membrane. Using a sharp paring knife, scrape off and discard all the white pith, leaving only the yellow zest. Tear the zest into roughly 1-inch (2.5 cm) pieces.

Slice the basil and roughly chop the parsley and combine in a bowl. Stir in the lemon pulp and juice and the lemon zest, then whisk in the olive oil and crushed peppercorns. Season to taste with salt.

Brush the hot plancha generously with olive oil (if cooking indoors, heat the griddle over medium-high heat, then brush with oil) and add the chickpeas in a single layer. Drizzle them with a few spoonfuls of the reserved broth and cook on one side only for a minute or two, until golden brown and crisp on the bottom. When the chickpeas are done, season them while still on the griddle with the vinegar and salt to taste. Transfer the chickpeas to a serving dish, add the onion and salsa, and toss well before serving.

FAINA, FOUR WAYS

This chickpea flatbread is a time-honored standby in Argentine pizzerias (in Uruguay, too). It's usually eaten as a first course while you are waiting for your pizza. In the old days, it was often made on a circular copper baking sheet that measured a full yard (meter) across. Copper is nice to have and beautiful to behold, but you'll get superb results with a cast-iron pan, too. As with pizza, there is a world of toppings you can serve with your faina. I often skip the pizza and make a meal of faina alone with briskly flavored toppings: choose from any one of my four favorite combinations (recipes follow). And, as always, feel free to follow your own culinary impulses.

Serves 4 to 6 as an appetizer

FOR THE FAINA

1 cup (92 g) chickpea flour

1 cup (237 ml) water

2 tablespoons extra-virgin olive oil

2 tablespoons freshly grated Parmesan cheese

½ teaspoon fine salt

Freshly ground white (as they use in Uruguay) or black pepper

Extra-virgin olive oil

1 small red onion, very thinly sliced through the root end

Grated zest of 1 lemon

A handful of fresh oregano leaves

To make the faina, place the chickpea flour in a bowl. Stir in the water and olive oil, then whisk vigorously until there are no lumps. Whisk in the cheese and season to taste with salt and pepper. Set aside.

Drizzle a teaspoon or so of olive oil onto a well-seasoned 12-inch (30 cm) rimmed cast-iron griddle or skillet and brush it around to liberally coat the surface and rim of the griddle. Heat the horno, or a home oven, to 450°F (230°C), putting the prepared griddle in the oven for 10 minutes to preheat it, too.

When the oven is hot, whisk the batter again. Using thick oven mitts, carefully pull the hot pan from the oven, oil it again, and pour in the batter, spreading it evenly into a large thin pancake. Bake for about 15 minutes, until the faina is set and the top is golden. Slip a spatula under it to loosen it, and slide it out of the pan onto a serving board.

Top with the sliced onion, lemon zest, oregano, and a drizzle of olive oil. Or choose one of the variations on page 226.

continued

VARIATIONS

FAINA WITH CASHEW, MANDARIN, AND BASIL SALSA

A mash-up of texture and taste, it's the sort of unruly combination that appeals to me.

½ cup (70 g) cashews

1 tablespoon extra-virgin olive oil

2 mandarin oranges

1 cup (30 g) fresh basil leaves

⅓ cup (10 g) fresh parsley leaves

¼ cup (59 ml) sunflower oil

Coarse salt and freshly ground black pepper

Make the faina as on page 225. Roughly chop half the cashews and reserve. Finely chop the remainder, add them to a mortar with the olive oil, and grind to a fine paste.

With a sharp knife, peel the mandarins down through the pith and membrane, then cut the segments out into a bowl with their juice. Chop the basil and parsley and add them to the mandarins, along with the chopped cashews and cashew paste. Whisk in the sunflower oil. Season to taste with salt and pepper. Spoon the salsa over the faina and serve the rest alongside in a bowl.

FAINA WITH PARSLEY, OREGANO, GARLIC, AND TOASTED SEED SALSA

Pungency, herbal notes, and crunchiness perk up the broad flavor of the faina.

1 cup (30 g) fresh parsley leaves, chopped

½ cup (15 g) fresh oregano leaves, chopped

1 garlic clove, minced

2 tablespoons toasted pumpkin seeds

2 tablespoons toasted sunflower seeds

1 tablespoon red wine vinegar

¼ cup (59 ml) extra-virgin olive oil

½ cup (118 ml) sunflower oil

Coarse salt

Crushed red pepper flakes

Make the faina as on page 225. Combine the parsley and oregano in a bowl with the garlic and toasted seeds. Whisk in the vinegar and oils, then add salt and red pepper flakes to taste. Spoon over the faina and serve.

FAINA WITH MUSHROOMS, GARLIC, AND PARSLEY

Most toppings that work on pizza often go well with faina.

½ pound (227 g) mushrooms, trimmed and sliced

3 tablespoons extra-virgin olive oil, plus more for the plancha

1 large garlic clove, finely chopped

½ cup (15 g) fresh parsley leaves, chopped

Coarse salt and freshly ground black pepper

Make the faina as on page 225. Place the mushrooms in a bowl with the olive oil, garlic, and parsley, and toss. Brush a hot plancha or skillet with oil. When it shimmers, add the mushrooms. Cook until the mushrooms start to brown, about 3 minutes. Season to taste with salt and pepper and spoon over the faina to serve.

LOCRO VEGANO WITH DRIED PEACHES

All along the flanks of the Andes, the Indigenous peoples on either side of the cordillera make a version of this recipe. Many cultures the world over mark important dates and holidays by sharing a traditional dish. In the United States, it's turkey on Thanksgiving. For Argentines, it's locro served on May 25, a day that marks the birth of our republic. Locro is made with squash, hominy, and beans. There are, of course, many variations of this ancient recipe, but almost all include the staples of the Indigenous larder: corn, beans, perhaps some tomatoes, and enough chile to rouse your palate. Although locro is usually made with some kind of meat, I don't think you'll miss it.

Serves 6 to 8

1 cup (200 g) dried hominy

1 cup (200 g) dried white beans

1 cup (200 g) dried chickpeas

3 ears fresh corn

⅓ cup (75 ml) extra-virgin olive oil

2 onions, chopped

8 garlic cloves, smashed and peeled

¼ cup tomato paste

1 large butternut squash, peeled, seeded, and cut into roughly 1½-inch (4 cm) pieces

8 cups (2 L) vegetable stock, plus more if needed

3 bay leaves

Coarse salt and freshly ground black pepper

1 teaspoon crushed red pepper flakes

2 tablespoons pimentón dulce (sweet Spanish paprika)

5 dried peaches, cut into quarters

FOR THE SALSA

1 or 2 bunches scallions

¾ cup (177 ml) extra-virgin olive oil

1 tablespoon pimentón dulce (sweet Spanish paprika)

½ ounce (14 g) fresh hot chiles, or to taste, sliced

1½ tablespoons red wine vinegar, or to taste

Soak the hominy, white beans, and chickpeas separately in bowls filled with plenty of water overnight.

Shuck the corn and cut each ear in half. Slice the kernels off three of the halves and set aside in a bowl. Slice the remaining halves into 1-inch-thick (2.5 cm) rounds and set aside with the kernels.

Prepare a fire for medium heat and set a grate over it. Pull out a large deep pot with a lid, such as a caldero or stockpot. Set the pot on the grate (or on the stovetop over medium heat if cooking indoors). Add ¼ cup of the olive oil, the onions, and the garlic to the caldero or pot and cook, covered, for several minutes, until softened but not browned. Stir in the tomato paste and cook for about 5 to 7 minutes, then add the squash and stir everything together. Cover and cook for about 8 minutes, or until the squash starts to soften.

Uncover the pot and stir, scraping up any browned bits from the bottom. Stir in the drained hominy, white beans, and chickpeas. Add the corn slices and kernels, then pour in the stock—there should be enough liquid to cover the vegetables; if not, add more stock. Add the bay leaves, then season to taste with salt and black pepper, the red pepper flakes, and the pimentón. Stir well, cover, and cook over medium-low heat for about 2 hours. It should cook at a gentle bubble. Every 15 minutes, give the locro a good stir, scraping up anything sticking to the bottom to make sure it doesn't burn, adjusting the heat if necessary, and breaking up the squash as it cooks. The squash will gradually break down completely and blend with the liquid into a creamy base for the beans. About 20 minutes before serving, add the dried peaches.

To make the salsa, cut off the green parts of the scallions, slice into thin rings, and place in a small bowl. Finely slice the white parts and set aside in a separate bowl. Warm the olive oil in a skillet over medium heat, add the pimentón and chiles, and cook until lightly browned. Remove from the heat and stir in the vinegar and the white parts of the scallions. Serve in individual bowls, with the salsa spooned over the top and sprinkled with the scallion greens.

HUMMUS MILANESAS
WITH CHERRY TOMATOES

When people think of Argentinean food, most likely the first thing that comes to mind is a beefsteak doused with chimichurri. But in fact, the one dish you are apt to find in every restaurant or bodega is a milanesa: a breaded beef cutlet. This recipe is a vegan approach that captures the idea of a milanesa with a tender crust of hummus atop grilled eggplant. Like a classic eggplant Parmigiana, this milanesa wants some tangy tomatoes. A salad of mixed herbs is a light but flavorful finishing touch.

Serves 4

FOR THE HUMMUS

2 garlic cloves, peeled

2½ cups (420 g) drained cooked or canned chickpeas

2 tablespoons fresh lemon juice

½ teaspoon salt

¼ cup tahini

2 to 3 tablespoons extra-virgin olive oil

1 globe eggplant

Extra-virgin olive oil

Coarse salt and freshly ground black pepper

6 cherry tomatoes, cut in half

2 large handfuls of fresh soft herbs, whole leaves, such as basil, parsley, coriander, and mint

Juice of 1 lemon

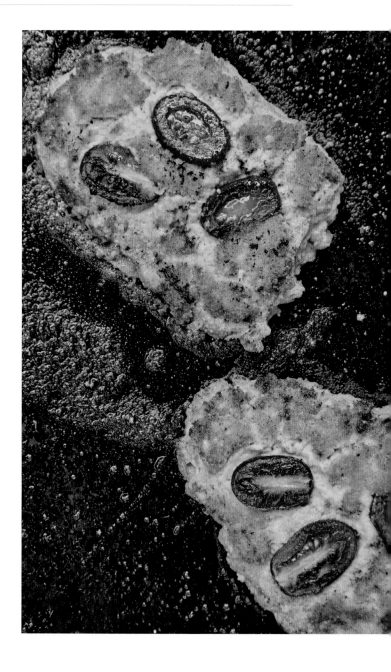

Prepare a fire for medium heat and warm the plancha. (Or pull out a large cast-iron griddle if cooking indoors.)

To make the hummus, put the garlic in the bowl of a food processor and pulse to chop. Add the chickpeas, lemon juice, salt, and tahini and pulse to combine. Gradually add the olive oil, pulsing until the mixture is well combined but still a bit coarse and (most important) thick and dense enough to hold its shape. Set aside.

Cut 4 even slices, about ½ inch (1.25 cm) thick, from the eggplant. Pat dry and lightly score both sides with a sharp knife. Brush both sides generously with olive oil and season to taste with salt and pepper.

Line a sheet pan with parchment paper. Scoop out one-quarter of the hummus, set it on the parchment, and shape it into a patty about ½ inch (1.25 cm) thick. Repeat with the remaining hummus. Gently press 3 cherry tomato halves, cut side up, into the top of each patty, patting the sides back in so the patties hold their shape. Set aside.

Generously brush the hot plancha with olive oil (if cooking indoors, heat the griddle over medium-high heat, then brush with oil). When the oil shimmers, cook the eggplant slices until golden brown on the bottom, about 5 minutes. Brush the tops with oil and turn to cook the other side for about 3 minutes, adding more oil if needed. They should be tender all the way through. Move to a cooler part of the plancha to keep warm, or transfer to a large plate and tent with foil.

Oil the hot plancha or griddle again and sprinkle the tomatoes with salt. Using a wide sharp-edged spatula, lift a hummus patty and in one quick motion flip it tomato side down onto the hot plancha or griddle. Repeat with the remaining patties, giving each one plenty of space. Cook the patties undisturbed until the tomatoes brown and a tender crust forms on the bottom of the hummus. With two wide spatulas (one in each hand), carefully turn the patties to brown the other side for about 3 minutes. At any time during the cooking, feel free to add a little more oil to the plancha or griddle if it seems dry.

Meanwhile, toss the herbs in a bowl with the remaining lemon juice.

As the milanesas are done, carefully lift them from the plancha and transfer onto the eggplant slices. Top with the dressed herbs and serve immediately.

PUMPKIN
AND SQUASH

THE OLD MAN AND THE GARDEN

Our next-door neighbors in Bariloche had a beautiful home that they would visit for a month in the summer and a few weeks during ski season. Their caretaker—who looked after the place the rest of the time—was a serious gardener whom we called Don Pedro as a sign of respect. In the summertime, he would start work on the garden at five a.m. every day and stay at it until the heat and sun were too intense, about ten a.m. He'd return to finish his chores late in the afternoon. Don Pedro was one of those people who could feel the life in things that grow in the ground and nurture it. His rhubarb was, as we say in Argentina, bárbaro (shorthand for "outrageously good"). He grew beautiful lettuces, plump cherries, sweet carrots, and miraculous raspberries. To this day, I have never found their equal. But if I close my eyes and summon up an image of him, I find him in his pumpkin patch in late autumn, when the green leaves of our Andean pumpkin vines have withered away and all that remain are brilliantly colored pumpkins.

"You must leave them connected to the earth as long as possible," he advised me, as if he were reciting an article of deep religious faith. "Until the frost comes, they will take nourishment from the soil and their flavor will become deeper and richer."

This is true of many of the squashes of autumn—butternut, Hubbard, acorn, and delicata. The longer you leave them on the vine before harvesting, the better they develop sugars that caramelize beautifully in the presence of fire. Roasted in the embers, these squashes become meltingly sweet. On the plancha or in the horno—cut into crescents—they brown and crisp on the outside. Their crumbly texture drinks up the flavors of butter, olive oil, vinegar, lemon. Fresh herbs stand out as islands of flavor.

Zucchini or summer squashes are a different story. They should be picked in season and are wonderful raw or caramelized on the plancha, but in this chapter I cook them on hot coals until they are charred and juicy.

WHOLE ROASTED BUTTERNUT SQUASH AL RESCOLDO WITH SALSA CRIOLLA

Imbued with a bit of smokiness, squash, when cooked rescoldo-style, is intensely sweet with a smooth mouthfeel. Laced with salsa criolla (a condiment we use almost as frequently as chimichurri), this recipe amounts to a duel between the immense sense of warmth and sweetness from the squash and the bright notes of onions, bell peppers, spices, and vinegar.

Serves 4

1 large butternut squash
Salsa Criolla (recipe follows)

Prepare a fire and let the charcoal burn down to a bed of embers, coals, and ashes for rescoldo. If cooking indoors, preheat the oven to 400°F (200°C).

Bury the squash in the embers. Cook until the squash is tender enough to be pierced all the way through with a long metal skewer, about an hour. When it is done, carefully remove it from the embers with strong, long-handled tongs and set aside to cool. If cooking indoors, place the squash in a large roasting pan and roast for about 1 hour, turning occasionally, until the squash is tender all the way through.

Once the squash has cooled, brush off all the ash and cut it lengthwise in half with a sharp serrated knife. Scoop out and discard all the seeds and stringy bits, and transfer the cleaned-up halves to a serving platter, cut side up. Spoon some salsa criolla into each cavity and over the top and serve the remaining salsa on the side.

Salsa Criolla

This much-loved salsa is rounded out by seasoning with cooled salmuera (saltwater brine).

Makes about 3 cups (712 ml)

3 bell peppers (1 red, 1 yellow, 1 green)
3 small ripe tomatoes, seeded and chopped
1 red onion, minced
3 tablespoons red wine vinegar
1 cup (237 ml) extra-virgin olive oil
Coarse salt or Salmuera (page 292)
Freshly ground black pepper

Halve the bell peppers and remove the stems, seeds, and the white pith. Slice into very fine strips, then chop. Combine the bell peppers in a bowl with the tomatoes and onion and mix well. Stir in the vinegar, then the olive oil, and season to taste with salt or salmuera and black pepper. Let stand for about 30 minutes to blend the flavors.

ROASTED BUTTERNUT SQUASH WEDGES WITH AJADA

When you roast squash wedges, you expose more of the surface of the squash flesh to caramelizing heat. Garlic-based ajada sauce is something I first ate in Seville at Expo '92, the 1992 world's fair. Spaniards often use it as a finishing touch for cooked fish, pouring the boiling vinegared sauce over the fish. Like many sauces, it diffuses into the food you put it on, so when you make a sauce and taste it for balance, remember that you have to think ahead to how it is going to taste with your squash. Ajada is also quite nice on cauliflower or potatoes.

Serves 4

1 butternut squash (about 2 pounds/1 kg)
3 tablespoons extra-virgin olive oil
Coarse salt and freshly ground black pepper

FOR THE AJADA
¼ cup extra-virgin olive oil
4 garlic cloves, thinly sliced crosswise
1 teaspoon Pimentón de la Vera
1½ tablespoons red wine vinegar

Heat the horno, or a home oven, to 400°F (200°C).

Cut the squash in half lengthwise with a strong serrated knife. Scoop out and discard the seeds and all the stringy flesh around them. Slice the halves lengthwise into evenly sized wedges about 1½ inches (4 cm) thick. Spoon half the olive oil onto a sheet pan, add the squash, and turn the wedges to coat thoroughly. Drizzle with the remaining olive oil, then season to taste with salt and pepper. Roast until browned and tender, about 10 minutes on each side. Arrange on a platter.

To make the ajada, heat the olive oil and garlic together in a small cast-iron skillet over medium-low heat. When the garlic begins to turn golden (in about a minute), remove the skillet from the heat and quickly stir in the Pimentón and vinegar. The mixture will bubble and hiss in the still-hot skillet. Immediately pour the ajada over the squash and serve.

ACORN SQUASH ROUNDS WITH AVOCADO

I rarely see avocados invited into a squash recipe, but it works very well. The squash is sweet and a bit nutty. The avocado is softer and creamier, much more subtle in taste. Throw in some herbs for accent, some nuts for crunch, and lemon juice for brightness, and this newly formed friendship will delight you.

Serves 6

3 medium acorn squashes
(about 1 pound/454 g each)
½ cup (118 ml) extra-virgin olive oil
3 lemons
3 avocados
Fleur de sel and freshly ground black pepper
¼ cup toasted sunflower seeds
A handful of fresh oregano leaves

Heat the horno, or a home oven, to 375°F (190°C).

Slice the unpeeled squash crosswise into rounds about ½ inch (1.25 cm) thick and discard the seeds and strings and end pieces. They will be a little uneven in diameter, but it doesn't matter.

Liberally coat one or more sheet pans with olive oil and arrange the squash rounds on the pan in a single layer. Brush the tops lightly with some of the olive oil. Roast for about 20 minutes, turning once, until golden brown outside and creamy inside.

Meanwhile, grate the zest of 1 lemon and set aside. Squeeze the juice from the zested lemon into a small bowl. Cut the remaining 2 lemons into wedges.

Halve, pit, and peel the avocados, and coat the exposed flesh well with the lemon juice to preserve its color.

When the squash is done, use a wide metal spatula to gently lift the rounds onto a large, wide serving platter. Arrange the avocado halves among the squash. Sprinkle with the lemon zest, season to taste with fleur de sel and pepper, and scatter the sunflower seeds and oregano over all. Serve with the lemon wedges on the side.

ROASTED CALABAZA STRIPS WITH DILL

The tastes of childhood linger with us throughout our lives. I have loved dill ever since I was quite young and would visit Ruth and Alfred von Ellrichshausen (see page 111). Ruth was a wonderful cook who ran a charming restaurant on the shores of Lake Nahuel Huapi. She was the type of cook who jealously guarded her cooking secrets, but by paying close attention to what she served, I learned my first lessons in the art of cheffing and creating the right atmosphere in a restaurant. Like many Northern Europeans, she was partial to dill, and I have used it ever since.

Serves 4 to 6

1 calabaza or other winter squash
(about 2 pounds/1 kg)
⅔ cup (157 ml) extra-virgin olive oil
Coarse salt and freshly ground black pepper
A large handful of dill sprigs, roughly torn

Heat the horno, or a home oven, to 375°F (190°C).

Cut the calabaza in half, then into quarters; do not peel. Slice the quarters as thinly as possible. Brush them with some of the olive oil.

Brush a large sheet pan with some olive oil and arrange the squash slices on the pan in a single layer. Brush them again with olive oil, season to taste with salt and pepper, and roast for 15 minutes or more, depending on the thickness of the squash, until golden brown and tender. Transfer the slices with a sharp-edged spatula to a serving platter, and gently push the slices up with your fingers to form ruffles. Check the seasoning, shower with fresh dill, and serve.

SQUASH A LA PLANCHA

I've always liked going into an old-fashioned diner or coffee shop in America for a breakfast of eggs, bacon, and some home-fried potatoes. This way of preparing squash reminds me of that: cubes of squash cooked on a griddle until they are soft on the inside and browned on all sides. The extra pleasure that squash affords is the caramelized sweetness of the browned parts. A sprinkling of thyme sends up an aroma that beckons you to dig in.

Serves 4 to 6

1 winter squash, such as kabocha or butternut (about 2 pounds/1 kg), peeled and cut into 1-inch (2.5 cm) cubes

3 tablespoons extra-virgin olive oil, plus more if needed

3 tablespoons fresh thyme leaves

Coarse salt and freshly ground black pepper

3 garlic cloves, minced

½ cup (118 ml) heavy cream

A large bunch of scallions, green parts only, sliced on the diagonal

Prepare a fire for medium heat and warm the plancha. If cooking indoors, heat a large cast-iron skillet over medium heat.

Toss the squash cubes on a sheet pan with 2 tablespoons of the olive oil.

Brush the hot plancha or skillet with the remaining 1 tablespoon olive oil. When the oil shimmers, spread the squash cubes on the hot surface in a single layer, working in batches and adding more oil as necessary. Cook the squash until browned and crisp on the bottom, about 3 minutes, then turn and cook until browned on all sides, about 5 minutes.

Add a tablespoon or two of water, quickly scraping it toward the center with a spatula and collecting any sweet browned bits from the pan. Continue cooking until the squash is tender, 5 to 10 minutes more, depending on the squash.

Season the squash with the thyme and salt and pepper to taste, then add the garlic and the cream, scraping it into the squash as it thickens into a sauce. Using two wide spatulas, transfer the mixture to a platter, scraping up the reduced cream along with the squash. Scatter the scallions over the top and serve hot.

ROUND ZUCCHINI A LAS BRASAS

Round zucchini—also known as Eight Balls—are nice cooked a las brasas (directly on the coals). It's important that these zucchini be medium size. Small ones will burn, and large ones are so full of water that the result can be bland. But a nice medium-size one chars beautifully, cooks through, and picks up some smoky nuance. You can also use regular zucchini or summer squash if they are sturdy enough to withstand the coals.

Serves 6

6 round zucchini

A handful of fresh mint leaves

About 5 tablespoons extra-virgin olive oil

1 tablespoon red wine vinegar

Fleur de sel and freshly ground black pepper

2 lemons, cut into wedges, for serving

Prepare a fire and let the charcoal burn down to a bed of embers, coals, and ashes for rescoldo.

Using long-handled tongs, set the zucchini directly on the coals. Cook, turning occasionally, until the skin is nicely charred in patches and the zucchini are tender and juicy when pierced with a long skewer, 7 to 10 minutes total, depending on the size of the zucchini. Lift them out with the tongs and set aside until cool enough to handle, then wipe off the ash with paper towels.

Cut the zucchini into quarters and arrange in a shallow serving dish. Shower with the mint, and dress lightly with the olive oil, vinegar, fleur de sel, and pepper. Serve with the lemon wedges on the side.

FRUIT

SIZZLE AND SWEET

There are few things that you can say hold true for every child, everywhere in the history of humanity, but I have yet to meet the young one who will refuse an invitation to pick and devour a ripe fruit. The same holds true for the child that remains in every one of us. It is one of the incomparable joys of summer to be able to pluck a grape off the vine, a blueberry off the bush, or a peach off the bough of a tree weighed down with plump yellow orbs: their rosy blush puts me in mind of a young woman applying a hint of rouge before going out for the evening. When ripe, every fruit reaches a perfect balance of sweetness and acidity.

Fire transforms fruit in a special way; the sugars in the part of the fruit that comes in direct contact with the heat caramelize and even burn in spots. Both effects can be delicious. Just beneath this first layer, the flavors in the fruity flesh intensify. Whenever I bring fiery heat to fruit—whether roasting, baking, grilling, or braising—I adore every variation of taste and texture in the communion of fruit and fire. I have a sweet tooth. But then, so do you.

GRILLED GRAPES WITH MELTED CHEESE

Whether served as an aperitif or a dessert, few combinations are more charming when dining alfresco than a bunch of grapes, brushed and burnished by fire and eaten along with cheese that you've melted moments before serving. As with wines made from different varietals, grape flavors vary, which gives you an opportunity to play sommelier and choose a pairing that balances the sweetness of fruit and the savoriness of cheese. For the cheese, I like to use Tetilla, a Spanish cheese from Galicia, but you can use Comté or something similar.

Serves 6

8 tablespoons (113 g) unsalted butter, cut into 1-inch (2.5 cm) pieces

1 cup (200 g) sugar

2 pounds (1 kg) red grapes, in large bunches

1 pound (454 g) cheese for melting, such as Tetilla or Comté

1 baguette, sliced

Prepare a fire for medium heat and warm the plancha. If cooking indoors, heat a cast-iron skillet or griddle over medium heat.

Add the butter to the hot plancha or skillet. When the butter melts, add the sugar. Roll the grapes around in the mixture to coat, then let them cook for a few minutes to caramelize in parts. Take the grapes off before they burn.

Meanwhile, set the cheese on a separate area of the plancha or on a second skillet, and as it melts, spoon it onto slices of bread to eat with the grapes.

STONE FRUIT GALETTES

When peaches, plums, apricots, and nectarines are in season, I adore burning them a bit before baking. Instead of the usual buttery pastry crust of a galette, these mini-galettes are made with a savory bread dough that soaks up all the juice from the fruit.

Note: Make the dough a day ahead of time and chill it.

Serves 6

FOR THE DOUGH

1¼ teaspoons active dry yeast

About 1¼ cups (275 ml) lukewarm water

4 cups (about 500 g) flour, sifted, plus more for dusting

1½ teaspoons fine salt

1 tablespoon plus 2 teaspoons sunflower oil, plus more for the pan

9 ripe nectarines, peaches, or plums or a combination, halved and pitted

¾ cup (150 g) sugar

4 tablespoons unsalted butter, cut into small pieces (optional)

Oil, for the pan

Fresh lemon balm leaves, for garnish

To make the dough, dissolve the yeast in 1 cup (237 ml) of the lukewarm water. Combine the flour and salt in the bowl of a stand mixer fitted with the paddle attachment and mix on low speed. Gradually add the yeast mixture and the oil and mix until the dough comes together, adding more water as needed by the tablespoon. Switch to the dough hook and knead on medium speed for about 5 minutes, until the dough is smooth.

Divide the dough into six portions, shape them into balls, and wrap them in plastic wrap. Refrigerate overnight.

Heat the horno, or a home oven, to 375°F (190°C).

Place the halved fruit in a bowl, add the sugar, and toss gently. Heat one or more large cast-iron griddles over medium-high heat until a drop of water sizzles on the surface. Working in batches, arrange the fruit on the hot griddle, cut side down, without crowding, and cook for about 3 minutes, or until browned. Turn and brown on the other side, adding pieces of butter around the fruit if desired, being careful to remove the fruit while it is firm enough to hold its shape. Set aside and let cool.

Brush a sheet pan with oil. Flour a work surface and roll out the dough into disks ⅛ inch (3 mm) thick. Working with one dough disk at a time, place three pieces of fruit in the center of the disk and pull the exposed dough up over the fruit, leaving the fruit uncovered in the center and forming pleats in the dough as you go. Transfer to the prepared sheet pan. Repeat with the remaining dough and fruit.

Bake the galettes for about 20 minutes, until they are golden brown. Garnish with the lemon balm.

ROASTED STRAWBERRIES WITH RICOTTA AND MINT

Strawberries have a strong affinity for dairy. The English adore their strawberries and cream while watching tennis players compete at Wimbledon. Strawberry shortcake with whipped cream is an American dessert classic. Eastern Europeans prepare blintzes with strawberries and farmer cheese. In this sumptuous dessert, I caramelize sugar, butter, and strawberries and spoon the molten stew over a dollop of ricotta topped with fresh mint.

Serves 6

2 pints (450 g) ripe strawberries

½ cup (113 g) sugar

4 tablespoons cold unsalted butter, cut into 6 pieces

1½ cups (300 g) chilled ricotta cheese

A handful of fresh mint leaves

Prepare a fire for medium-low heat and set a grate over it.

Hull the berries and place in a bowl. If they are large, cut them in half lengthwise. Add the sugar and gently toss the berries to thoroughly coat.

Pour the berries into a 9- or 10-inch (23 or 25 cm) cast-iron skillet and dot with the butter. Set the pan on the grate (or on the stovetop over medium heat) and cook until the sugar melts and the berries begin to caramelize, 3 to 4 minutes. Stir occasionally as the butter melts into the caramelized sugar and berries and forms a sauce. Remove the pan from the heat and strain the sauce into a bowl, leaving the berries in the warm skillet. Return the pan to the heat to brown the berries for a minute or so.

Spoon the ricotta onto a serving dish and top with the roasted berries. Shower with the mint and serve the warm sauce on the side.

GRILLED BIZCOCHUELO WITH ROASTED STRAWBERRIES AND ICE CREAM

Bizcochuelo is a simple sponge cake briefly dipped in syrup, grilled in butter, and served with a scoop of vanilla ice cream. A finishing touch of roasted strawberries delivers just the right balance of acid and sweetness to pull all the flavors together.

Serves 8

FOR THE BIZCOCHUELO

Butter and flour, for the pan

4 eggs, at room temperature

¾ cup (150 g) sugar

1 teaspoon fine salt

1 teaspoon vanilla extract

¾ cup (100 g) cake flour, sifted

Vegetable oil, for the plancha

1½ cups (354 ml) Simple Syrup (page 299)

8 tablespoons (113 g) unsalted butter, at room temperature

½ cup (100 g) sugar

Roasted Strawberries (page 257)

2 pints vanilla ice cream (store-bought or homemade)

To make the bizcochuelo, heat the horno, or a home oven, to 350°F (180°C).

Butter and flour an 8-inch (20 cm) square cake pan. Line the bottom with a piece of parchment paper cut to fit, and butter and flour the parchment.

Break the eggs into the bowl of a stand mixer fitted with the whisk attachment and add the sugar and salt. Beat at high speed until it doubles in volume. Add the vanilla and beat until the mixture forms a ribbon when the whisk is lifted. Remove the bowl from the mixer and, using a silicone spatula, gently but thoroughly fold in the sifted flour in three batches. Pour the batter into the prepared pan and bake for 20 to 25 minutes, until the top is golden brown and a skewer inserted into the center comes out clean. Set the pan on a wire rack and let the cake cool for about 10 minutes in the pan, then unmold onto the rack and cool completely.

Prepare a fire for medium-high heat and warm the plancha. (Or pull out a large cast-iron griddle if cooking indoors.)

Cut the cake into quarters and cut each quarter into 1-inch-thick (2.5 cm) slices. Lay the slices out on a sheet pan.

continued

Pour the simple syrup into a wide shallow bowl and, using tongs, quickly dip the slices of cake into the syrup and return them to the pan. Don't let them soak up too much syrup or the cake will fall apart. Cut half the butter into small pieces, and gently spread onto the cut sides of the cake, then sprinkle with sugar. Set aside.

Warm the roasted strawberries.

Oil the hot plancha or griddle over medium-high heat. Lay the cake, buttered side down, on the hot surface and cook until nicely browned, about 2 minutes. As the cake caramelizes, dot more butter around it so it doesn't burn. Turn and repeat on the other side, dotting with more butter as needed.

To serve, set four slices of cake on a serving plate. Top two of them with ice cream and roasted strawberries, and cover with the other slices of cake. Eat immediately, while the berries are warm and before the ice cream melts.

VANILLA ICE CREAM WITH OLIVE OIL AND SEA SALT

A few years ago, Andrew Schlesinger, one of my most gifted culinary students (also a tremendously successful entrepreneur), was traveling through Italy when he had the notion to douse his ice cream with sea salt and fresh cold-pressed olive oil. These two ingredients bring forward the unctuousness and salinity that is often masked by the overpowering sweetness of ice cream. It's always quite marvelous to see how a few simple ingredients—in this case savory ones—can reveal nuances in an old favorite like vanilla ice cream.

Serves 4

4 cups (946 ml) store-bought vanilla ice cream
4 teaspoons (20 ml) extra-virgin olive oil
Fleur de sel

Divide the ice cream among four serving bowls. Spoon 1 teaspoon of the olive oil over each and sprinkle with fleur de sel to taste.

PLANCHA PEACHES, PLUMS, AND CHEESE

As plums cook, they dissolve into a thick syrup. Peaches develop an enchanting crust. You want a cheese that crusts up well while staying quite soft inside. Try your favorite semi-firm cheese and see how it works. I have had success with semi-firm goat cheeses, but also Gouda, Cantal, and Raclette.

Serves 4

2 peaches, halved and pitted

2 plums, halved and pitted

2 tablespoons sugar

¼ cup extra-virgin olive oil

4 tablespoons unsalted butter, cut into pieces

½ pound (227 g) semi-firm melting cheese, sliced ½ inch (1.25 cm) thick

Prepare a fire for medium-high heat and warm the plancha. If cooking indoors, heat a large cast-iron griddle over medium-high heat.

Sprinkle the cut side of the peaches and plums with the sugar. Brush the hot plancha or griddle with some of the olive oil, then melt the butter on it. Add the fruit, cut side down, then cook until browned on the bottom and starting to soften slightly, about 3 minutes. Move the fruit to the edge of the plancha to keep warm. If cooking indoors, move the warm griddle off the heat—the retained heat will keep it warm.

Adjust the coals for high heat, or increase the stove heat to high, to grill the cheese. Drizzle the plancha or another griddle with more olive oil and arrange the slices of cheese on it. Grill without disturbing the cheese until a coppery crust forms on the bottom, about 1 minute.

With a wide, sharp-edged metal spatula, carefully scrape up and turn the slices of cheese to cook on the other side. If the cheese is already melted, you won't need to flip it. When the cheese is crusted on the bottom, transfer to a serving dish and spoon the warm fruit and juices around it. Serve immediately.

BURNT GRAPEFRUIT, CAMPARI GRANITA, AND MASCARPONE

London's River Café was my gastronomic home whenever I found myself in England. The partnership of Rose Gray and Ruth Rogers was an ever-flowing source of delicious ideas and simple modern elegance. They used to make a ruby grapefruit granita that was a superb palate cleanser. Here, as elsewhere, grapefruit can't seem to make up its mind whether it wants to be sweet or bitter. Campari, likewise, combines these two fundamental and disparate flavors. A dollop of mascarpone serves as a creamy unifier. The flavor washes over me like a ripple of paradise arising in a dream.

Serves 6

FOR THE GRANITA

¾ cup (150 g) sugar

About ½ cup (118 ml) water

4 cups (1 L) fresh grapefruit juice

½ cup (118 ml) Campari liqueur

6 pink grapefruits

1 cup (200 g) sugar

8 ounces (225 g) mascarpone cheese, plus more if desired

To make the granita, combine the sugar and water in a small saucepan. Bring to a boil over medium heat and cook for 5 minutes. It should be clear and syrupy. Remove from the heat and let cool.

In a bowl, combine the grapefruit juice and Campari. Whisk in the cooled syrup and pour into a shallow freezer container, preferably metal. The mixture should be about 1 inch (2.5 cm) deep in the container. If necessary, you can use two containers. Cover with plastic wrap. Place in the freezer until the granita is evenly frozen, scraping the frozen edges in toward the center with a fork every 30 minutes, giving the granita a crystallized appearance. It should take about 2 hours, depending on your freezer.

Heat the horno, or a home oven, to 475°F (245°C).

Slice the ends off the grapefruits with a sharp knife. Then slice off and discard the peel, cutting all the way down through the pith to expose the flesh.

Place the sugar in a bowl, add the whole grapefruits, and roll them around in the sugar to coat. Set them on a sheet pan and roast for 5 to 10 minutes, until the sugar caramelizes. Let cool.

Serve the grapefruits at room temperature with the granita and mascarpone.

BURNT CHERRIES AND ICE CREAM

This is part performance art and part dessert. I enjoy making this, eating it, and most of all beholding the looks of astonishment from guests as I place a hot cast-iron skillet on a bowl full of ice cream topped with sugar-dusted cherries. Everyone holds their breath as I wield the hot iron. Trepidation gives way to smiles, as the sweet clouds of burnt sugar, singed ripe cherries, and vanilla notes of the ice cream meet. Few things are certain in this life—the impact of this dessert is one of them.

Use pot holders!

Serves 6

2 pints (946 ml) vanilla ice cream

10 ounces (280 g) cherries, halved and pitted

4 tablespoons sugar, plus more if needed

A handful of fresh mint leaves, for garnish

At least 8 hours before serving, pack the ice cream into a 5-cup (1 L) heatproof and freezer-safe serving bowl or other container, cover, and place in the freezer.

Half an hour before serving, take the bowl of ice cream out of the freezer so the ice cream softens a little. Combine the cherries and 2 tablespoons of the sugar in a bowl to macerate. Prepare a fire for medium-high heat, set a grate over it, and heat a cast-iron skillet on the grate. If cooking indoors, heat it on the stovetop over medium-high heat.

Arrange the cherries in a layer on top of the ice cream and sprinkle them evenly with the remaining 2 tablespoons sugar. Using a heavy-duty pot holder, position the hot skillet over the cherries and lower it onto them for about 10 seconds, or until the sugar melts and caramelizes the cherries. Set the hot pan aside. The caramelized cherries will melt into the ice cream and soften it enough to scoop it into individual serving bowls. Garnish with the mint.

WATERMELON SALAD WITH HERBS, TOASTED HAZELNUTS, AND CRACKED BLACK PEPPER

This dish is a dessert with overtones of an appetizer. The watermelon dominates the visual but is not overpowering. It is fresh and sweet, happy to play with mint and/or any herbs that strike your fancy. I toss in some cheese and nuts, too.

Serves 6

One 5-pound (2.3 kg) watermelon
A large handful of arugula
A large handful of fresh mint
A large handful of fresh lemon balm or any other herb

4 ounces (113 g) shaved cheese, such as a young fresh pecorino or aged goat cheese
½ cup (113 g) toasted hazelnuts (page 297)
Extra-virgin olive oil
Juice of 2 lemons
Fleur de sel
Cracked black peppercorns

Using a large spoon or ice cream scoop, scoop the watermelon out of its rind and arrange it on a large platter. Scatter the arugula, mint, lemon balm, cheese, and nuts all around it. Dress lightly with olive oil and the lemon juice, and season to taste with fleur de sel and cracked pepper.

WHOLE ROASTED PINEAPPLE WITH BLUEBERRIES

Fruits are so delicate and evanescent that they rarely benefit from long cooking. But pineapples—just like a rib roast—can cook for a long time. When I cook them on a dome (see page 149), I hang them for hours, but you can also cook them, as I do here, on the grill and obtain lovely results in less time. Think a young wine versus aged Burgundy: they both have their virtues, but with a different investment of time.

Serves 6

2 cups (475 ml) water

2 cups (400 g) sugar

1 ripe pineapple

1 tablespoon vegetable oil, plus more if needed

3 cups (435 g) blueberries

3 cups (710 ml) vanilla ice cream

Prepare a fire for medium heat and set a grate over it. If cooking indoors, preheat the oven to 375°F (190°C).

Meanwhile, make a syrup. Pour the water into a saucepan and add the sugar. Set over medium heat and cook, stirring occasionally, until the sugar dissolves. Pour into a deep roasting pan just large enough to hold the pineapple.

Slice off the bottom and the sides of pineapple and trim out the eyes. Lay the pineapple down in the hot syrup and turn to soak all sides.

If cooking outdoors, brush the grate with oil. Lay the pineapple down on one side and grill until nicely caramelized, about 15 minutes. Pick it up with a set of tongs, dunk it in the syrup to thoroughly drench it, and return it to the grill to brown on the second side. Grill for at least an hour, dunking it in the syrup every 15 minutes and returning it to the grill until all sides are browned and the pineapple is tender. You should be able to poke a bamboo skewer all the way through when it's done (it will put up slight resistance at the core).

If cooking indoors, lay the pineapple on its side in a second roasting pan and put it in the oven. Every 15 minutes, take it out and roll it in the syrup to baste. When it is tender all the way through and very juicy but still holding its shape, transfer it to a cutting board to rest for 5 minutes before serving.

To serve, divide the blueberries among six serving plates. Crush half of them with the back of a fork, leaving the rest whole, and top each portion with a scoop of ice cream. With a long serrated knife, carve the pineapple into thick rounds and stand one slice upright on its side in each serving of ice cream.

SALT-BAKED PEARS
WITH STAR ANISE SYRUP

I have been making this recipe since my earliest days of restaurant cooking with fire. Even though the pears are baked in salt, they are not terribly salty—just enough to balance the sweetness of the cooked fruit. People always like to see the mounds of salt, not really knowing what to expect when you crack the salt crust, releasing the irresistible perfume of the baked pears. You can eat them as is or with a Camembert or other soft ripened cheese.

Serves 4

FOR THE SYRUP

2 cups (475 ml) water

1 cup (200 g) sugar

1 teaspoon cardamom pods

1 teaspoon coriander seeds

1 strip orange zest

1 strip lemon zest

3 star anise pods

1 cinnamon stick

3 pounds (1.5 kg) coarse salt

4 large, ripe Bosc pears

The day before serving, make the syrup. Pour the water and sugar into a small saucepan and heat over medium heat. When the sugar has dissolved, remove the pan from the heat and add the cardamom, coriander, orange zest, lemon zest, star anise, and cinnamon stick. Let steep for 24 hours.

The next day, heat the horno, or a home oven, to 425°F (220°C).

Pour the salt into a large bowl. Gradually add water by the cupful, mixing it into the salt with your hands until it reaches the consistency of damp snow.

Make a bed of damp salt on the bottom of a small roasting pan. Arrange the pears about 1½ inches (4.5 cm) apart and cover them completely with the remaining salt, mounding it up in between and around them and leaving only the stems exposed so you know where they are. Bake for 45 minutes.

Cover a heatproof work surface with newspapers. Remove the roasting pan from the oven and set it on the newspapers. Crack the salt crust lightly with a rolling pin, taking care not to smash the pears. Using a long-handled serving spoon, lift off and discard the big pieces of salt. As the pears are exposed, whisk off the remaining salt with a pastry brush.

Meanwhile, warm the syrup over medium-low heat.

Cut the pears in half and serve in individual bowls topped with a spoonful of syrup and with the remaining syrup on the side.

COCKTAILS

BETTERED BY BURNING

Cocktails are a carefree pleasure. They mark a kind of border: between the concerns of the day and a time to refresh your spirit after your toils. I am very specific about how I like to consume a cocktail. I especially like to sip it in the convivial atmosphere of a bar: The maraca sound of ice in a shaker. The precision with which a skilled bartender makes just enough to fill a coupe exactly to the rim, neither *one* drop more nor less. The way the oils gently spray out from a twist of lemon rind and lie on the surface of the liquid. The view in the mirror behind the bar, where your reflection can keep you company. The softly spoken words of a couple in love, looking deeply into each other's eyes and talking as if they are all by themselves, neither noticing nor caring about anything but each other. The anticipation as you watch the bartender fill your glass. And then, of course, that first sip, as you assay the intricate blending of aroma and flavor. At this point, I usually decide that for this moment at least, all is right with the world. "Nothing to excess and everything in proportion" was the motto of the artists and architects of the Athenian Golden Age. I feel the same way about cocktails; they should be just enough to stimulate but not overwhelm your senses. The trend to serve cocktails in a glass as big as a goldfish bowl is good neither for romance nor the full enjoyment of a meal.

As you'll see in this chapter, my tastes in cocktails run to the time-tested favorites. It has taken years and years for them to reach their place in the mixologist's Holy Scriptures. Adding a little bit of smoke and fire to them delivers a subtle nuance in the same way that a gifted musician might linger on a pause in a Chopin polonaise. So when you are grilling at home or gathered around the fire pit, use the flames to char an element for your cocktail: a lime garnish, an orange twist, or even a slice of papaya. A little char or smokiness adds another layer to your drinks. Most of these recipes are made for one, but they are easy to double or expand for more when guests arrive.

PISCO SOUR WITH BURNT LIME

Pisco is a liquor made from distilled wine. Both Peru and Chile claim it as their invention, since pisco was first made by the Spaniards who brought wine grapes to their new colonies. To sidestep this passionate debate, I observe that pisco is basically brandy and that the conquistadores in both countries knew very well how to distill wine. So I will come down firmly in the middle and credit both countries.

The well-known (in South America) soft drink known as Brazilian lemonade incorporates the whole lime (skin, pith, flesh, and all). My pisco cocktail calls for scorching a lime, which tamps down the bitterness of the rind; less bitter . . . more better.

Makes 1 drink

1 lime
1 ounce (30 ml) pisco
½ ounce (15 ml) Simple Syrup (page 299)
1 egg white
8 to 10 ice cubes

Prepare a fire for medium heat. Chill a cocktail glass.

Using long-handled tongs or a kitchen fork and wearing an oven mitt, hold the lime over an open flame, rotating it occasionally as it softens and chars in patches. This should take about 5 minutes. Let it cool, then slice off and discard both ends and pare off a piece of lime zest to save for garnish.

Place the whole lime and the pisco, syrup, egg white, and ice cubes in a blender and blend on high until the lime is puréed and the mixture is foamy. Strain into the chilled glass, garnish with the burnt lime zest, and serve.

GIN AND TONIC WITH BURNT LEMON AND CUCUMBER

In the main, I like to sip a cocktail, but a gin and tonic is all about taming my thirst in the heat of summer. I confess to gulping this and perhaps coming back for another round. The clear gin, the bubbly tonic, and plenty of ice create a heat-relieving winterscape in my mind as I sit and sip in my T-shirt, shorts, and sandals.

Makes 1 drink

1 slice lemon

1 slice cucumber

1 ounce (30 ml) gin

3 ounces (90 ml) tonic water

Prepare a fire for medium heat and warm the plancha. If cooking indoors, heat a cast-iron skillet or griddle over medium heat.

Set the lemon and cucumber slices on the hot plancha or skillet for a minute or two until lightly charred but still juicy.

Pour the gin and tonic over ice in a tall glass. Garnish with the burnt lemon and cucumber.

BOURBON AND BURNT CHERRY SOUR

Bona fide bourbon, by the laws of the state of Kentucky, must be made in charred oak barrels that are used only once. After that, many of the barrels are sold to Scotch whisky makers who have no compunction about using and reusing the barrels to impart a smoky taste to their liquor. Use a good bourbon to make this smoky cocktail.

Makes 1 drink

4 cherries

1 tablespoon sugar

2 ounces (60 ml) bourbon

1 ounce (30 ml) fresh lemon juice

Prepare a fire for medium heat and warm the plancha. If cooking indoors, heat a small cast-iron skillet or griddle over medium heat.

Cut the cherries in half around the pit, so that the stem remains intact on one side. Leave the pit in place or remove it, if desired. Gently roll the cherries in the sugar.

Place the sugared cherries cut side down on the hot plancha or skillet and cook them without moving until they are nicely caramelized, about a minute. Be careful not to let the sugar burn! Lift them off onto a plate with a sharp-edged spatula as soon as they are done.

Measure the bourbon and lemon juice into a cocktail shaker and shake well to combine. Pour into a cocktail glass over ice and garnish with the burnt cherries.

CITRUS AND POMEGRANATE COCKTAIL

I served this drink—sweet, citrusy, with an extra punch of tanginess—at my beach restaurant, Chiringuito, in the town of José Ignacio in Uruguay. It is so refreshing on a hot summer's day, on the beach or at a backyard cookout. It goes down easy . . . pace yourself.

Serves 4

2 large mint sprigs

1 pomegranate

1 bottle rosé wine

1 cup (237 ml) Simple Syrup (page 299)

Juice of 2 lemons

Juice of 2 oranges

Juice of 2 grapefruits

Slices of lemon, orange, and grapefruit, for garnish

Prepare a fire for medium heat and warm the plancha. If cooking indoors, heat a small cast-iron skillet or griddle over medium heat.

Place one of the mint sprigs on the hot dry plancha or skillet just until it chars slightly, 1 minute or less. Remove and set aside.

Cut the pomegranate in half crosswise and remove the seeds from one half. Set aside. Cut the remaining half into 4 slices for garnish.

Pour the wine, simple syrup, citrus juices, charred and fresh mint, and pomegranate seeds into a pitcher. Stir well, bruising the fresh mint with the spoon to release its flavor, and add plenty of ice. Garnish with the sliced citrus and pomegranate and enjoy.

NEGRONI WITH BURNT ORANGE

Ernest Hemingway drank Negronis, as did James Bond. Negronis are hugely popular in Buenos Aires, where some bars dispense them from spigots, just like beer on draft. Some years ago, Ruth Gray, the wonderful, and sorely missed, chef of London's River Café, was writing her cookbook and asked me for a Negroni recipe. My mind went immediately to the ice-cold, sweet, bitter, and shyly powerful version that they serve in the Hotel Hassler in Rome. There was little to do by way of improvement other than share this information with Ruth. While thinking about cocktails for this book, I burnt an orange slice in hopes that it would add a grace note to the traditional recipe. I expect you will agree.

Makes 1 drink

1 orange slice

½ ounce (15 ml) sweet red vermouth, preferably Carpano Antica Formula

½ ounce (15 ml) gin

½ ounce (15 ml) Campari

Prepare a fire for medium heat and warm the plancha. If cooking indoors, heat a cast-iron skillet or griddle over medium heat.

Set the orange slice on the hot plancha or skillet and let sit until it is lightly charred but still juicy, about a minute.

Place some ice cubes in a cocktail glass and add the vermouth, gin, and Campari. Stir, then garnish with the burnt orange slice.

PAPAYA SLUSH

There is an old jazz tune, sung by Rosemary Clooney, where she promises "papayas, anything your heart desires." This slushy drink picks up the spirit of her song. Look for a ripe, sweet papaya—the grilled garnish is addictive.

Makes 1 drink

1 slice unpeeled ripe papaya, for burning

3 (1-inch/2.5 cm) cubes of peeled ripe papaya

1 ounce (30 ml) vodka

3 ounces (90 ml) papaya juice

½ ounce (15 ml) Simple Syrup (page 299)

Prepare a fire for medium heat and warm the plancha. If cooking indoors, heat a cast-iron griddle or skillet over medium heat.

Set the papaya slice on the hot plancha or griddle and grill until the bottom is charred in patches, about 1½ minutes. Using a sharp-edged spatula, turn it over and repeat on the other side. Set aside.

Combine the cubed papaya, vodka, papaya juice, and simple syrup in a blender with crushed ice. Blend until the papaya is smooth and the mixture is slushy. Pour into a cocktail glass and garnish with the grilled papaya.

SCORCHED MINT MOJITO

Cocktail culture, which went hand in hand with sophisticated nightclubs and clientele as seen in the movies of the 1930s and '40s, represented a glamorous life that people longed for as economic hard times and war enveloped the world. Two of the most fertile centers of cocktail invention were Buenos Aires and Havana. The mojito was created in Cuba, the offspring of its vast sugarcane fields and world-class rum. It was a specialty of Havana's Bodeguito del Medio, a welcoming dive bar that still retains its vintage charm. My version substitutes brown sugar and dark rum for refined white sugar and light rum, giving it a more robust flavor that holds its own when paired with scorched mint.

Makes 1 drink

1 lime slice

2 mint sprigs

2 tablespoons turbinado sugar

1 lime wedge

1 ounce (30 ml) dark rum

½ ounce (15 ml) Simple Syrup (page 299)

½ ounce (15 ml) fresh lemon juice

Prepare a fire for medium heat and warm the plancha. If cooking indoors, heat a small cast-iron skillet or griddle over medium heat.

Place the lime slice and 1 mint sprig on the plancha or skillet just long enough to lightly char them, a minute or less. The mint will char more quickly than the lime; be careful not to burn it too much and dry it out.

Place the sugar on a cutting board. Rub the lime wedge around the rim of a cocktail glass, then turn the glass upside down and place it in the sugar to coat the rim. Pour the rum, simple syrup, and lemon juice into the glass. Add the fresh mint and press on the leaves and stem so that the liquid picks up the mint flavor. Add ice and garnish with the burnt mint and lime.

BASICS

SALMUERA

This is the saltwater brine that gauchos use to baste their meat, but I started using it many years ago to season oil-based salsas and vinaigrettes. Here is the basic salt and water formula:

1 tablespoon salt to 1 cup (237 ml) water

Bring the salt and water to a boil in a small saucepan and stir until the salt dissolves. Cool the solution and use to season other ingredients for a condiment. Store tightly covered in the refrigerator for up to a week.

MY BASIC VINAIGRETTE

This has been my basic for years. And of course, there are endless ways to vary it—a new olive oil or vinegar, a spoonful of Dijon mustard or chopped shallot, any herb imaginable.

Makes 1 cup (237 ml)

2 tablespoons red wine vinegar

½ teaspoon coarse salt, dissolved in 1 teaspoon boiling water to make a salmuera

½ teaspoon freshly ground black pepper

6 tablespoons extra-virgin olive oil

Place the vinegar, salmuera, and pepper in a medium bowl. Whisk to combine. Add the olive oil in a slow, steady stream, whisking continuously to form an emulsion. Store tightly covered in the refrigerator for up to a week.

CHIMICHURRI

Traditionally served with steak, chimichurri adds a kick to almost any grilled vegetable. Make it a day or so in advance to give the flavors a chance to blend. Refrigerate it in a mason jar and shake it well just before serving.

Makes about 2 cups (475 ml)

1 cup (237 ml) water

1 tablespoon coarse salt

1 head of garlic, cloves separated and peeled

1 cup packed (30 g) fresh parsley leaves

1 cup (30 g) fresh oregano leaves

2 teaspoons crushed red pepper flakes

¼ cup red wine vinegar

½ cup (118 ml) extra-virgin olive oil

Prepare a salmuera by bringing the water to a boil in a small saucepan. Add the salt and stir until it dissolves. Remove from the heat and let cool.

Mince the garlic and place in a bowl. Finely chop the parsley and oregano and add to the garlic with the red pepper flakes. Whisk in the vinegar, then the olive oil. Whisk in the salmuera and transfer the mixture to a jar with a tight-fitting lid. Store in the refrigerator; shake before using.

PARSLEY, GARLIC, AND OLIVE OIL SALSA

This Argentine condiment enlivens just about anything it touches and is ready in a minute. I often add a bit of lemon confit or zest if I have it and spoon it over any grilled vegetable or even a bowl of fresh noodles with grated cheese.

Makes about 1 cup (237 ml)

1 cup packed (30 g) fresh parsley leaves, finely chopped

2 or more garlic cloves, minced

⅓ cup (78 ml) extra-virgin olive oil, plus more if desired

Coarse salt and freshly ground black pepper

Place the parsley in a small bowl, then add the garlic. Gradually whisk in the olive oil until it reaches the desired consistency. Season to taste with salt and pepper. Store tightly covered in the refrigerator for up to a week.

AIOLI

My version of the Provençal classic. Serve with grilled vegetables.

Makes about 1 cup (237 ml)

2 egg yolks, at room temperature
2 garlic cloves, peeled
Coarse salt
About 1 cup (237 ml) light extra-virgin olive oil, or part olive oil and part vegetable oil

Set a mixing bowl over a folded towel to keep it steady, then add the egg yolks.

Grate the garlic over the egg yolks with a Microplane. Add a pinch of salt, then whisk well to combine.

Whisking constantly, add the oil a few drops at a time, then by tablespoons, until the yolks thicken and emulsify. Whisk in the remaining olive oil in a slow, steady stream, until the oil has been incorporated and the aioli is smooth and thick. Store tightly covered in the refrigerator for up to 3 days.

VEGAN MAYONNAISE

Make this vegan mayo with aquafaba, the liquid from canned chickpeas.

Makes about 1½ cups (354 ml)

6 tablespoons aquafaba
1½ tablespoons fresh lemon juice
2 teaspoons Dijon mustard
½ cup (118 ml) plus 1 tablespoon extra-virgin olive oil
½ cup (118 ml) plus 1 tablespoon vegetable oil

Measure the aquafaba, lemon juice, and mustard into a blender jar. Blend for about 1 minute, until foamy. With the motor on, gradually add the olive and vegetable oils in a thin, steady stream and blend until the mixture is thick and shiny. Store in the refrigerator for about a week.

VARIATION

VEGAN AIOLI
Add 1 or 2 grated garlic cloves to the Vegan Mayonnaise.

SUN-DRIED TOMATOES

Not remotely like the ones you can buy, these tomatoes are paper-thin and jewel-like. We slice ours on a deli slicer and dry them on the sunny rooftop of my restaurant in Garzón. At home, you can slice them on a mandoline and dry them in a sunny window or even over a radiator. Store them in olive oil and pick out a few to garnish a salad, or make a little panini of them with a bit of cheese and some fresh basil leaves.

Makes about 2½ cups (590 ml)

4 or 5 large, firm plum tomatoes, not too ripe
About 2 cups (475 ml) mild olive oil

Line several sheet pans with silicone baking mats, rough side facing up. Slice the tomatoes crosswise paper-thin on a mandoline, then carefully lay the slices out in rows on the mats. Don't worry about the seeds—they will dry along with the rest of the tomato.

Set the trays out in the sun to dry for a day, depending on the weather, or place the trays over or near a radiator. The edges will start to curl up, but when they are completely dry, the tomatoes will be flat, crisp, and delicate. One at a time, carefully lift them off the mat with a fine-edged spatula and arrange them in an airtight container or jar, then cover them completely with olive oil and seal the container. Store in the refrigerator for a week or more.

FRESH TOMATO REDUCTION

Simplicity itself, this is what I make when I have too many tomatoes and they're going soft. They barely cook, just reduce in their own juices to the purest essence of tomato. It freezes well, too, offering a welcome taste of summer long after the tomatoes are gone.

Makes about 2 cups (475 ml)

2 pounds (1 kg) ripe, juicy tomatoes, cored
Coarse salt and freshly ground black pepper
A pinch of sugar

Put the tomatoes in a saucepan over low heat and season very lightly with salt and pepper. Break them up with a metal spatula, add the sugar, and let them very slowly simmer in their own juices, tending to them occasionally with the spatula, until they have reduced by two-thirds. The more gently you cook it, the better the flavor will be. Don't worry about the seeds or skin; the long cooking softens everything. Refrigerate, tightly covered, for several days or freeze.

ORANGE CONFIT

The same idea as the lemon confit seen throughout the book, orange confit is equally refreshing. Use it to brighten up salsas; you can even brown the preserved zest along with vegetables right on the plancha.

Makes about 1 cup (237 ml)

2 oranges

1 bay leaf

6 whole black peppercorns

1¼ cups (295 ml) extra-virgin olive oil, plus more if needed

2 tablespoons dry white wine

1 teaspoon coarse salt

Cut the oranges in half. Squeeze out and reserve the juice. Put the squeezed halves in a saucepan and add the bay leaf, peppercorns, 1 tablespoon of the olive oil, the wine, and the salt. Add enough water to completely cover the oranges, then bring to a boil. Reduce the heat and simmer for about 20 minutes, until the orange peel is very tender. Remove from the heat and let cool in the liquid.

Drain the orange peel and tear it into rough strips about 1 inch (2.5 cm) wide. Set a strip of peel skin side down on a cutting board and, with a sharp paring knife, scrape off every bit of bitter white pith, leaving only the orange zest. Repeat with the remaining peel.

Put the strips of orange zest in a small airtight container and cover completely with the remaining olive oil. The confit will keep in the refrigerator for at least a week.

CRISPY GARLIC CHIPS

This appetizing topping brings a crisp garlicky punch to salads and soups. The chips are easy to make, but make sure you don't burn them—they cook in about 10 seconds!

Serves 4 to 6 as a garnish

10 garlic cloves, peeled

1 cup (237 ml) olive oil, for frying

Using a sharp knife or a small mandoline, slice the garlic very thin. Line a plate with two paper towels.

Heat the olive oil in a 10-inch (25 cm) cast-iron skillet over medium-high heat and watch it carefully. When the oil is very hot, test the temperature by adding a slice of garlic. If it sizzles, add the rest of the slices. They should become crisp and golden in about 10 seconds. Use a flat, slotted skimmer to keep them from sticking together, and remove the garlic slices the moment they turn color to drain on the paper towels. (The oil can be strained and reserved for another use if it is not burned.)

CRUNCHY BREADCRUMBS

Never throw out leftover bread. Instead, tear it into croutons while it's still malleable and fry it up with good olive oil. Use as is, or crush into finer crumbs, if you like. Keep it on hand to add crunch to salads, soups, or pastas.

Makes about 2½ cups (200 g)

8 ounces (200 g) day-old bread

About 3 tablespoons extra-virgin olive oil, plus more as needed

Coarse salt and freshly ground black pepper

Crumble the bread by hand over a bowl. Line a small sheet pan with paper towels. Warm the olive oil in a skillet over medium heat. Add the breadcrumbs and fry them for about 2 minutes, turning occasionally, until they are crunchy and browned to your liking. Add more olive oil if needed. Season to taste with salt and pepper. Transfer to the prepared sheet pan to drain. Store in an airtight container.

TOASTED NUTS

Almonds and walnuts are ready to use once they are toasted, but hazelnuts require one additional step to remove their bitter skins. Use toasted nuts in salsas, salads, or anywhere you need a bit of flavorful texture.

Makes 1 cup (125 g)

1 cup almonds, walnuts, or hazelnuts

Preheat the oven to 350°F (180°C).

Spread the nuts on a sheet pan. Bake for about 5 to 10 minutes, tossing occasionally, until the nuts are fragrant and toasted. If cooking almonds or walnuts, slide them right off the hot pan and onto a plate as soon as they are done to stop the cooking. For hazelnuts, slide them onto a clean dish towel and use it to vigorously rub off as much of the skins as you can. Use the nuts while still warm or store them in an airtight container.

VEGETABLE STOCK

This is a rich stock to use in polenta, soups, or braised dishes. The greater the vegetable-to-water ratio, the richer the stock. Add mushrooms, if you like, for even more body.

Makes about 4 quarts (4 L)

1 head of garlic, cut in half crosswise

2 large leeks, split, thoroughly washed, and cut into 2-inch (5 cm) pieces

6 celery stalks, quartered

2 medium onions, quartered

3 medium carrots, quartered

12 whole black peppercorns

2 bay leaves

Coarse salt and freshly ground black pepper

Put the garlic, leeks, celery, onions, carrots, peppercorns, and bay leaves in a large stockpot and cover with about 5 quarts (5 L) water. Bring to a boil, reduce the heat to low, and cook, partially covered, for about 1 hour. Add salt, tasting carefully, and pepper if you think it needs it.

Strain through a sieve into a large bowl, pressing down hard on the vegetables and garlic with a wooden spoon to extract all the flavor. Discard the solids. Taste again and adjust the seasoning. Refrigerate or freeze.

CLARIFIED BUTTER

You can cook with butter at higher temperatures if you melt it and strain out the milk solids. Use clarified butter as an alternative to olive oil for frying breadcrumbs or breaded vegetables.

Makes about 1½ cups (354 ml)

1 pound (454 g) unsalted butter

Place the butter in a small heavy saucepan and melt it slowly over low heat. Do not stir. Remove from the heat and skim off and discard the foam. Line a small fine-mesh strainer with cheesecloth and set it over a small bowl. Strain the butter through the cheesecloth into the bowl, leaving all the milk solids behind. Cool the strained butter and use immediately or store in an airtight container in the fridge for 2 weeks.

CHILE OIL

Keep a small jar in the fridge to use whenever a dish needs a kick. Choose any flavorful dried chiles, and add more or less olive oil to taste. Let the mixture steep for a day or two before using.

Makes about 1 cup (237 ml)

1 cup (237 ml) extra-virgin olive oil
5 whole dried chiles: 2 left whole, 3 crushed

Pour the olive oil into a small, lidded glass jar. Add the whole and crushed chiles. Shake well, cover tightly, and store in the refrigerator.

SIMPLE SYRUP

Use this liquid sweetener for mixed drinks or desserts. Use it plain, or flavor it by adding whole spices or herbs while it's warm and letting it steep for a while.

Makes about 1½ cups (354 ml)

1 cup (200 g) sugar
1 cup (237 ml) water

Combine the sugar and water in a small saucepan over medium heat. Cook, stirring, until the sugar is dissolved. It will keep for about a month refrigerated in a tightly covered container.

TIME

Quite early one morning, as the sun came up, I stepped outside with a blanket wrapped around me and my mug of coffee in my hands. I looked out at the landscape. Mist swirled as it rose off the valley floor, like brushstrokes on the hills. Still half in dreamland, I was reminded of the great Japanese painter Hokusai. Whether he painted a wind-lashed scene of country folk making their way through a downpour or two lovers entwined in an erotic fantasy, he was a master of a personal style, born of a tradition—but unmistakably his style alone. One thought of his has stayed with me. When he was seventy, though revered and respected, he said, "I feel like I am slowly becoming a good painter."

Then when he was eighty, he said, "I'm really painting well now, but I will be my best when I am ninety."

I have been cooking since I was a teenager, and only now do I fully understand what Master Hokusai meant. In my case, as a young cook, I wanted to learn everything, to try everything, but as time sped by, the things I learned that weren't really me slipped away, until I became—as we all do—someone unique and different.

In a manner of speaking, I grew younger inside as I aged.

That has been true of my work as well. Standing silently, all by myself, tending my fires, I came to realize that the secret of cuisine is often to do less but better. Maybe when I'm eighty I will still be a chef who wakes up each morning, looking at the hills, still eager to make love to life.

I have been washed by the years.

RESOURCES

CUSTOM GRILLS

If you are cooking with wood fire and would like a more professional setup, North Fork Ironworks makes a wonderful Argentine-style parrilla grill that we used for testing many of the recipes in this book.
northforkironworks.com

TUSCAN GRILL

For an inexpensive cast-iron setup for cooking with wood fire, many manufacturers offer low-to-the-ground Tuscan grills. As gauchos have done for centuries, you build your fire to one side and add coals under the grill as needed. Steve Raichlen makes a very good one.
stevenraichlen.com

WEBER KETTLE GRILL

Many of you may have the classic 22-inch (55 cm) Weber kettle grill. To adapt it for cooking my recipes with charcoal, I find the following quite useful: a pair of char baskets and a hinged cooking grate.
weber.com

CAST IRON

For cast-iron griddles, planchas, Dutch ovens, and skillets, Lodge offers the widest range of options, and their products are durable and high-quality.
lodgecastiron.com

AGRADECIMIENTOS

Lia Ronnen for unwavering support and the will to take chances. Judy Pray—always resolute, unfailingly cheerful. Donna Gelb for her magical and meticulous way of interpreting my recipes for the home cook. Peter Kaminsky for his friendship and the poetry of his prose. William Hereford, because he is an artist. Diego Irrera—no one knows the soul of my cooking more than he does. Ricky Motta—when he wields a knife at the chopping board, I know everything will be all right. Sebastian Benítez, who brings joy and color to every kitchen. Emilia and Florencia Pereyra & Pereyra for their laughter and precision. Bodega Garzón—her vines, her wines, her flavors! Colinas de Garzón—I can't live without your olive oil! Bodega Escorihuela, for a quarter century of sharing hope. Maria de Luynes, for her many years as my assistant and now the empress of The Island. Nicole Tuvi, who moves like a knife through water, getting everything done. Brendan McCarthy for his glorious and simple North Fork Grills. Julia Fleisch, Justine Garcia, Marta Matos, and Joanne Edelstein for their careful and honest recipe testing and tasting. Dick and Barbara Moore, who generously shared their Brooklyn backyard for the photo shoot, and Patsy Taylor, who made her apartment available for the photography team. Janet Mendel for steering us to ajada. Adrian Perez, the beating heart of Garzón. Olga Grigorenko, prop stylist, who always has the thing that is needed. Alejandro Conde and Diego Salaberry, who get it done. Martin Sosa—so proud to have seen you grow into who you are. Susana Pérez—you are the joy of our restaurant, always smiling. Nilda Rodríguez Muñeca—for her, everything is always possible. Sebastian García—so thankful for your cocktail wizardry. José Luis, for our ten years together. The strong young arms of Leo Zolberg and Ezra Septimus. The beautiful team at Artisan: editorial production, copyediting, and proofreading by Zach Greenwald, Paula Brisco, and Ivy McFadden; the design team of Suet Chong, Nina Simoneaux, and Maggie Byrd; Nancy Murray for book production; and Allison McGeehon for leading the publicity efforts. And to the team in Argentina, who shepherded this project for four years: Juan Ignacio Boido, Mariano Kairuz, Salomé Azpiroz, Isaías Miciu, and Johnatan Pavés. Dear Ann Bramson, who brought my work to Artisan and the United States. And, of course, Vanina Chimeno, for being my eyes, my love, and my courage. A todos mis hijos for letting me walk at the edge of uncertainty.

INDEX

Note: Page numbers in *italics* refer to photographs.

Library of Congress Cataloging-in-Publication Data is on file.

ISBN 978-1-64829-072-5

Design by Suet Chong

Artisan books are available at special discounts when purchased in
bulk for premiums and sales promotions as well as for fund-raising or
educational use. Special editions or book excerpts also can be created
to specification. For details, contact the Special Sales Director at the
address below, or send an e-mail to specialmarkets@workman.com.

For speaking engagements, contact speakersbureau@workman.com.

Published by Artisan
A division of Workman Publishing Co., Inc.
225 Varick Street
New York, NY 10014-4381
artisanbooks.com

Artisan is a registered trademark of Workman Publishing Co., Inc.

Printed in Canada on responsibly sourced paper

First printing, April 2022

10 9 8 7 6 5 4 3 2 1